PRAISE FOR
Heavenly Alliance

"*Heavenly Alliance* is a transformative guide to connecting with your spirit guides, angels, and ancestors. Through practical exercises and inspiring stories, Samantha Fey empowers you to manifest your dreams and live a life of purpose and joy. A must-read for anyone seeking to deepen their connection with their spirit-guide team and live a fulfilling life!"

—George Lizos, bestselling author of
Protect Your Light and *Secrets of Greek Mysticism*

"Samantha Fey has written a must-read primer for anyone seeking a richer relationship with their spiritual path."

—Ophira and Tali Edut (The AstroTwins),
resident astrologers for *ELLE* magazine and the authors of
more than twenty books, including *The Astrology Advantage*

"*Heavenly Alliance* is a delightful guide full of important information for those of us who want to develop a deeper relationship with our guides and angels, while also fostering an appreciation for life's challenges, blessings, and miracles."

—Jacob Cooper, LCSW, bestselling author of
Life After Breath and *The Wisdom of Jacob's Ladder*

"Reading *Heavenly Alliance* is like being handed a course syllabus for learning to be a student in this school called Earth. This is a rare book that will help bolster your passions, deepen your connection to spirit, and provide you with tools to navigate your life."

—Deborah Blake, author of *Everyday Witchcraft* and *The Goddess Is in the Details*

HEAVENLY ALLIANCE

Heavenly Alliance

Call On Your Spirit Guides, Ancestors,
and Angels to Manifest the Life You Want

SAMANTHA FEY

HAMPTON ROADS

This edition first published in 2024 by Hampton Roads
Publishing, an imprint of Red Wheel/Weiser, LLC
With offices at:
65 Parker Street, Suite 7
Newburyport, MA 01950

Sign up for our newsletter and special offers by going to
www.redwheelweiser.com/newsletter

Cover design by Sky Peck Design
Cover image by iStock/fcscafeine
Interior by Timm Bryson, em em design, LLC
Typeset in Adobe Jenson Pro

ISBN: 978-1-64297-061-6
Library of Congress Cataloging-in-Publication Data available
upon request.

Printed in the United States of America
IBI
10 9 8 7 6 5 4 3 2 1

CONTENTS

CONTENTS

ACKNOWLEDGMENTS

This book was born out of my desire to demonstrate how beautiful life is even in its darkest moments and to help readers understand the enormous power of love that resides within us that we can call upon to become master co-creators of our lives. With that in mind, I have to acknowledge the fantastic listeners to my podcasts. Your questions, stories, and insights inspire me more than words can express. I'd also like to thank my co-hosts and friends Deb Bowen and Denise Correll for their friendship and support. Thank you to my first cheerleader in this world of writing, Lisa Hagan. You knew I had this book in me, and for that I remain eternally grateful. Thank you to the wonderful team at Hampton Roads Publishing.

Thank you to my sisters and friends for supporting me through this writing journey. A very special thank you to Michael Pawlewicz. Your love has breathed new life into my world and inspires me every day.

And, as always, everything I do is for my three daughters, Olivia, Victoria, and Chloe. Thank you for your infinite love and enthusiastic cheers of: "You've got this, Mom!" I hope my love, words, and work remind you that you can do anything, be anything, and create the life of your dreams.

INTRODUCTION:
YOU ARE NEVER ALONE

In the spring of 2005, I experienced a profound spiritual awakening that eventually led me to leave my teaching career and embark on a brand new path that I believe was pre-planned before my birth. Oddly, it all started with a rock.

At the time, I was teaching English at a local community college. I loved my job, but I had a difficult student in one of my classes who kept sliding notes under my door that contained threatening messages like: "Today I went looking for your house. Tomorrow I will find it." I went to my department chair for help, but received little. One afternoon, I returned to my office after class and discovered a reddish-orange, kidney-shaped rock sitting on my desk. I always kept my door locked, so I wondered how this stone had ended up inside the locked office.

I hurried up four flights of stairs to the geology department and asked one of the teachers if he could identify the rock. He held it in his hand and said: "Oh yes, that's a nice piece of red jasper. Jasper is said to offer protection. Why do you need protection?" When I told him about the strange student who was scaring me with unwanted attention, he replied: "Then carry this with you." I think I might have rolled my eyes before muttering a thank you and returning to my office. A rock? How could a rock protect me? Still, I figured it couldn't hurt and began carrying the stone with me. Two weeks later, the student was arrested on unrelated charges and never returned to class. Suddenly, I was fascinated by rocks.

A few months later at a crystal show, a woman walked up to me and told me she had a message from my guides and asked to share it with me. When I nodded, she said: "Your guides want you to know that you're a healer. You're supposed to be teaching people about their own healing and intuition. You have to start with Reiki."

"Ray what?" I asked, thinking she was trying to sell me something.

"Reiki," she replied. "It's a form on hands-on healing. Check it out."

The next day, I stopped at a local metaphysical store to buy a book on crystals and saw a sign by the cash register advertising a Reiki class. I signed up and felt instantly drawn to this healing modality. The teacher told us that we had to meditate for twenty-one days to allow the new Reiki energy to take root within us. I'd never meditated before, but decided to give it a try. Suddenly, my intuition popped open. I started having more precognitive dreams.

I knew a friend was pregnant weeks before a test confirmed it. I started seeing flashes of colors around people. And it all terrified me.

When I was growing up, I had often seen ghosts and spirits. I knew things about people without knowing how or why. I dreamed about things that later came to pass. When I was sixteen, I awoke one evening to see a man with a long grey beard wearing a brown robe tied at the waist with a rope. He didn't say anything to me. He just stood at the foot of my bed and smiled. He was not transparent like some of the ghosts I'd seen as a child. He was fully present and standing uninvited in my room. I sat up in bed, squeezed my eyes shut and prayed: "I don't know why I see or sense these things, dear God, but it scares me. Please make it stop." When I opened my eyes, the man was gone. I spent the next fourteen years trying to fit in and be normal. Now I was afraid that all that weirdness from my childhood was coming back.

Then I began having recurring dreams that my husband at the time, a policeman, was going to be shot in the line of duty. When this precognitive dream came to fruition, I finally decided to surrender to my soul's truth. I told God/Creator/Divine Spirit that I was ready to follow this path. My husband was still in a coma, and the doctors were trying to prepare me for his death—something I refused to accept. So I struck a bargain with God, praying: "If you let my husband live, I will accept this strange intuitive world and go wherever you lead me." It must have worked, because, despite the doctors' dire prognosis, he lived. I signed up for intuitive-development classes and eventually left my teaching career to host a podcast dedicated to helping fellow intuitives learn to recognize, accept, and surrender with gratitude to their true soul plan.

The main message I try to share with listeners is that there's a reason why we're here. Our souls have important lessons to learn and beautiful gifts to teach and share with the world. Everything we've experienced, overcome, and persevered through has a purpose. And even though it can often feel lonely here on Earth, especially when we're going through difficult challenges, we have our ancestors, our guides, and our angels to call upon for assistance.

In this book, I hope to open you up to the amazing truth that *you are never alone.* Moreover, there is a reason you are here, living the life you are living. You have a purpose that was defined for you long before you were born. There is a plan that directs your life. And with the help of your ancestors, your guides, and your angels, you can discover that plan and manifest that purpose.

This book is intended to help you discover your own soul plan. Through stories, research, and real-life examples, I show you how to recognize that plan, follow it, amend it, and fulfill it. Each chapter contains information that can help you map your journey of discovery and ends with exercises that can help you along the way. My dearest wish is that what you find in these pages will lead you to manifest your true soul purpose here on Earth, and to help others manifest theirs.

PART I

Your Heavenly Alliance

———

CHAPTER I

Your Soul Plan

Dear Soul,

Congratulations! Your application to the University of Earth has been approved. Although this is the hardest school in which to succeed, your soul has proved ready to tackle the challenges, pitfalls, and enormous lessons that only the University of Earth can teach you. It is only here that you can learn to grow your soul. You will not be given a manual or any instructions while enrolled here. However, you will have the help of spirit guides, ancestors, and angels who will silently, but persistently, guide you on your path.

While preparing for your birth, your team of allies will assist you in creating your soul plan. This will include everything you're supposed to learn and teach while on Earth. You will also choose your parents, siblings (if you feel they're required), potential partners, mentors, friends, and career(s). Of course, immediately upon your birth, you will forget all of this, which is why *it's imperative that you stay in tune with your heart, your true inner self. This is your connection to your soul and your allies. Pay attention to signs, synchronicities, and divine timing. And be alert for your own intuitive nudges that will guide you along the way.*

We wish you the best of luck in your studies.

ONE NIGHT DURING THE LONELY, ISOLATING, CON-fusing times of the recent pandemic, Stephanie, one of my listeners, found herself tossing and turning when she remembered something I had said on my podcast: "If you can't sleep, say a prayer for someone." She decided to give it a try and said a prayer asking that anyone who needed positive energy would feel surrounded by love and support. The strategy seemed to work and she was soon fast asleep.

In the morning, when she checked her email, she was surprised to discover a new message from someone she didn't know. The message was addressed to "Stephanie" and the email address was correct. But the writer had clearly intended to send this private communication to someone else. Stephanie was shocked to discover that it came from a teenage girl who had written a suicide note explaining why she was thinking of ending her life.

Stephanie instantly wrote back to the young girl explaining that the email had somehow mistakenly been sent to her. Then she added her own story detailing her personal experience with suicidal thoughts when she was a teenager. She kept reminding the girl: "It gets better. I promise." She ended the message by telling the teen that she'd fallen asleep praying for someone, anyone, who needed her prayers to feel surrounded by love and support, then pointed out that there was something bigger than us all, bigger than we can conceive, that loves us and wants the best for us. The two continued to correspond and Stephanie happily reported that the girl changed her mind about ending her life and was doing much better.

What unseen force guided Stephanie's prayers that night? How had this young teenager mistakenly sent her email to someone who'd dealt with the same issues she was facing when she herself was young? Could this all be a random coincidence?

I'm sure you've heard the old adage: "You're born alone and you die alone." But stories like Stephanie's prove this is not true. You are not alone on this journey. You have a team of invisible allies on the other side who have dedicated their time, wisdom, and love to supporting you as you work your way through this school of life. You can call them angels, guides, ancestors, universal loving energy—the label doesn't matter. What is important is that you learn to trust, solicit, and expect this love and support with joyful gratitude.

Your team of allies is constantly trying to communicate and connect with you, but you have to learn their language. You have to recognize the signposts along the way and be ready to take action on the directions they give you. Sure, it would be great if you could just call them up or dash off an email asking for explicit instructions and insights. But you exist here under the law of free will, which means that you have to ask for help and then act on it when the help is offered. The key is to be able to recognize the assistance you are given, which often comes through intuitive nudges, signs, and synchronicities, or a consistent feeling that something isn't right.

There Are No Coincidences

Let me share a personal example to illustrate how subtle and, at the same time, how obvious the messages from our guides and helpers can be. When I was fourteen, my dad finally admitted that he had a drinking problem and checked himself into a rehab center. On my first visit to see him, I was shocked to see a wing of the building dedicated to teens in recovery. I walked by patients who were just a little older than I was sitting in circles under the warm June sun, laughing and talking with their sponsors. And then I heard a little voice in my head say: "Pay attention. This place will be important to you one day." I had no idea what that intuitive message meant.

Years later, when I was a senior in college, I found that I was unsure of my next steps as graduation day loomed closer. I had majored in history and wanted to pursue a graduate degree, but I knew that I first needed to get a job and save money. I had applied to a few master's programs, but I'd also been offered a job that would enable me to take a break from school and live with friends. One day, my advisor called me into her office and told me about a master's program that offered the option of working as a substitute teacher during the day without pay, in return for which my tuition would be forgiven. This meant I could go to school at night and remain free of school debt, so I decided to apply.

A few weeks later, I received a phone call from the principal of a small, alternative high school asking me to come for an interview. I was not excited at the prospect, especially when I realized that the school consisted of three rooms attached to the back of a run-down church that was in need of a paint job. I can still remember the sound of my heels clicking on the well-worn laminate floor as if my shoes were agreeing with me: "No, no, no."

But the second I shook hands with the principal, I felt a sense of warmth and welcome. I couldn't shake the voice whispering in my head: "You belong here." "No, I don't," I kept silently repeating to myself. "I belong in the city with my friends, not this rundown, sad building." And then the principal asked me if I had any experience with addiction. I paused a moment and answered that my father had been in AA for eight years, and that my mom and I attended Al Anon meetings The principal nodded and told me that the students I'd be teaching there had either just been released from jail or from— you guessed it—the same rehab center where I had visited my dad! Suddenly I knew that, after four years of perfect freedom, I would be moving back home to spend my days teaching in this church and my nights attending graduate school. It would be hard, grueling work. But I knew this was my path.

I felt a rush of adrenaline coursing through me as I left the interview, having already accepted the job. This was in the days before cell phones, but I had to tell someone, so I pulled over to a pay phone and called my best friend. When she answered, I shouted into the phone: "Have you ever felt as if God were actually talking to you? As if your path had just been laid out before you like a shiny yellow brick road, and you knew there was no other choice?" She waited a beat before asking: "Samantha, what in the hell are you talking about now?" I laughed and said: "I'm going to grad school!"

While in college, I had changed my major three times. I had no idea what I wanted to do with my life. I prayed for help and guidance, but it felt as if no one was listening. On my last night before heading back to school after summer break, knowing that I had to

Your Soul Plan
declare a major and having no idea what to do, I woke
He rubbed his eyes and sat up groggily, then asked me:
"What's your favorite subject?" "History," I answered
in that and go back to sleep," he said with a yawn. And

During those years, if you'd asked me if I had guides,
answered with a firm "no." Yet looking back, I see that all
these things lined up to bring me to that meeting with

The answer is simple. This is how our team of invisible
allies operates to steer the course of our lives. Their care-
But it's always there, helping us discover our soul plans.
We just have to open our eyes and ears and minds to their

But before we dive into who your allies are and how you
can connect with them for a deeper, richer life experience,

let's first take a look at who *you* are and how you got here. And, most important, where you are heading.

Mapping Your Soul Plan

Each of us comes into this life with a specific set of goals we're here to accomplish, lessons we need to learn and teach, challenges we must overcome to grow in strength and love, and karma that needs to be healed and resolved. And before we're born, we meet with our team of allies to map out the plan by which we will lead our lives.

Picture a conference table surrounded by people who truly know and love you. Now visualize a screen on which a media presentation of your prior lives is projected. As you look through your past incarnations and make notes of your accomplishments—and, more importantly, areas where you failed to meet your goals—your team helps you craft your soul plan. Through these meetings, you and your team identify the lessons you must learn, the challenges and opportunities you will encounter, and the purpose you are meant to fulfill. Each of us comes into this life with a specific set of goals we're here to accomplish, lessons we need to learn and teach, challenges we must overcome to grow in strength and love, and karma that needs to be healed and resolved.

The next step in creating your soul plan is to choose your family. You will choose your parents and carefully coordinate the circumstances in which you will be raised. This is the foundation of the curriculum you will follow in the school of life. You may choose wonderful parents to help support you on your journey. Or you may select parents who are incapable of affection to help you learn self-love.

Then you must determine what you want to teach others during your life on Earth. Writer and speaker Wayne Dyer believes that, before he was born, God asked him what he wanted to teach in his life. He answered: "Self-reliance." To which God responded: "Then we'll have to give you a father who will abandon you and be such a bad father figure that you will be forced to learn self-reliance yourself. Only then can you teach it." And in fact, Dyer was passed from one abusive father to another. Finally, despite the inner rage he felt—or perhaps because of it—he found the seeds of forgiveness in his heart. In retrospect, he realized that his painful childhood experiences ultimately taught him resilience and self-reliance.

When you examine the family you were born into from this perspective, you begin to see the beautiful and sometimes painful lessons your soul is meant to learn. What did your parents teach you about love, security, and safety? How has this shaped your views on life? What impact did their love or lack of love have on your life as a child and as an adult? How did your childhood experiences make you stronger, more self-reliant, and capable of sharing love? What did your parents teach you about who are you and how you matter in this world?

We're all teachers and students for each other. Like the grain of sand that turns into a pearl under stress or the chunk of coal that emerges as a diamond under pressure, you transform into your true light when you encounter relationships that push your buttons, break your heart, and cause you to fall apart momentarily. When you are able to put yourself back together, you are different—stronger and shining brightly like a diamond, with the innocence and grace of a pearl at the core of your heart.

Working from this foundation, you and your spiritual team then map out the helpful people and mentors you'll meet along your journey who will guide you toward discovering your soul purpose. You choose your friends, teachers, partners, co-workers, and family members. Your guides show you signposts—often in the form of synchronicities or divine timing—that serve to remind you that you're on the right path. You also choose your challenges—those dark nights of the soul that enable so much growth and strength to blossom in your heart.

Your soul plan is like a map for your life journey. But this does not mean that everything is predetermined. A blueprint for building a house rarely comes to fruition exactly as planned. There are always unforeseen changes and challenges. The budget isn't big enough for the kitchen counters you want. The paint colors you chose don't match the living room furniture you love. Instead of bead board in the bathroom, you now want wallpaper. Things change and evolve. And the same thing happens as you follow your soul plan. It's just a map that suggests the people, situations, and experiences your soul needs in order to grow. This is very clear in the story of a client named Meg.

Meg's Map

Meg was a strong, confident, outspoken woman who was raised by a Marine dad and a stay-at-home mom who eventually became a fitness trainer. She was born to be tough and strong. In high school, she started to notice that her hands tingled when she was around sick people. When she was in college, she went along with some friends who were having psychic readings done, although she didn't believe in the mumbo-jumbo. When the woman told Meg she was a healer and would eventually be able to see auras and chakras, she stubbornly scoffed at the prediction. But she kept it to herself that she did often see hazes of color around people. She also didn't tell anyone that she carried a jade crystal in her pocket wherever she went, because she felt it gave her good luck. Meg was holding on to her identity as a tough, strong, no-nonsense woman.

When she became a nurse, Meg earned a reputation for accurate diagnoses and often had to use her strong personality to battle with doctors who "knew better." Once, when she was changing a dressing, she felt what she called "her second set of hands" sinking into the patient's abdomen. She sensed a blockage there and saw a glowing orange circle right next to it. She didn't know at the time that she was seeing and sensing the sacral chakra. When she asked the doctor to do another scan of the patient's abdomen, she was shocked when it showed that a piece of surgical swabbing had been left there. That's why the patient wasn't healing as quickly as expected.

Still, throughout her life, Meg ignored all these signs and kept stubbornly pushing through her days at the hospital. An ugly divorce and a bout with depression led her to pursue meditation. This quiet reflection gave her the determination to study the chakras, the human aura, and other healing modalities. Shortly after her six-tieth birthday, she retired from nursing and now works as a healer. She believes it's what she was meant to do all along, and often criticizes herself for refusing to see the signs she received throughout her life.

She may be right. It may well be that it was in her soul plan to be an intuitive healer right from the start. But that's the thing with soul plans. They eventually lead you to where you need to be. If you take the scenic route, that's okay. If you choose the road with potholes, traffic, and construction delays, that's okay too.

And Meg might be wrong. It may be that it was part of her soul plan all along to be a nurse, to meet her first husband, and to use these experiences to learn that true strength comes from accepting yourself exactly as you are. If soul plans are like maps, then it's important to remember that landscapes can change. So go easy on yourself. There's always room for change, growth, and improvement.

Test Days

Once your soul plan is complete and you get to this school of Earth, you exist here under the law of free will. This means that you have the right to accept or reject the help your allies give you and to alter those plans. Remember, life is a school. And in school, you are always tested to determine how much you have learned. That's how you evolve and grow.

Think back to when you were in school sitting at your cramped, tiny desk hunched over a test, with the sound of a slowly ticking clock heightening your anxiety as you tried to remember that quadratic equation you learned in algebra class. If you raised your hand and asked the teacher to refresh your memory, she wouldn't do it. That's what the test is for—to see if you learned it on your own. And this is how it works with your team of allies as well.

But this is where many start to lose faith in their teams. You have to learn to recognize which moments in your life are test days, because it is during these challenging times—when you feel you need your team the most—that they must be silent. If your teacher had reminded you what the answer was, you might have passed the test, but what would you have learned? Nothing.

The key to working with your team of allies is to rely on them for help and support consistently throughout your life, while also utilizing the skills, resources, and abilities you've cultivated within yourself to navigate life's pitfalls, choices, and divergent paths successfully. Inside of you is a treasure of untapped resources that can assist you on your journey. And your soul knows the way. Your soul knows why you're here.

Light Lessons: Three Envelopes

Before you can connect with your team of allies, you have to know how to embrace your own inner knowing. This exercise can help you tune in to and trust your own personal intuitive guidance without doubt or judgment. Many find it difficult to trust their inner knowing because they question or doubt the information that comes through. This simple exercise will help you develop trust in the still, small voice within you without your own opinions filtering through.

For this exercise, you will need three identical envelopes, three identical index cards, and a pen or pencil.

1. Sit comfortably and put yourself into a meditative state. Imagine roots emerging from the soles of your feet and going through the floor beneath you, down into the ground.

2. Visualize your energy opening and expanding. See your energy reaching up, up, up through the skies, just as your roots are reaching down, down, down into the earth. Breathe deeply throughout this process.

3. On each of the index cards, write a question on which you want information or guidance. Place each card in a separate envelope, then shuffle the envelopes and place them in front of you.

4. Pick up one envelope and close your eyes. Don't open it; just hold it and pay attention to what you feel. On the outside of it, write down what you are feeling and sensing.

5. Now focus on any emotions, words, or songs that pop into your head and write them on the envelope. Direct your attention to what you see and add any images, symbols, pictures, or scenes that appear in your mind's eye.

6. Then just sit with the envelope between your hands and ask your helpers: "What do I need to know about this situation?" Write down whatever comes to you.

7. Put the envelope aside and pick up the next one. Repeat these steps, then continue on to the third envelope.

8. When you are finished, open the envelopes, read your questions, and see how your answers correspond. Record your responses in your journal so you can refer to them later.

CHAPTER 2

Your Spirit Guides

Dear Soul,

Throughout your studies at the University of Earth, you will be assigned several guides to help you along your way. One main guide will be with you throughout your time here, but other guides will come and go as their help is needed with your various life lessons and challenges. These guides are familiar with your unique soul plan, with your individual gifts and talents, and with the obstacles you'll encounter as you journey through life.

As per the guidelines of the university's rigorous curriculum, you will not be able to see or converse with these guides, but there are several ways you can connect with them for help and additional insight. Please read the syllabus below to understand the best ways in which to link with these helpers.

MANY RELIGIONS AND CULTURES HAVE LONG believed in spirit guides. The ancient Greeks believed in a guardian *daemon*—not to be confused with a Christian demon—an elevated being who assists in our decisions, interpreting human concerns to the gods and in turn delivering divine messages to us. These minor deities or evolved humans are mentioned repeatedly in Greek literature, for instance in Plato's symposium, where a priestess tells Socrates that love is actually a highly evolved daemon.

Plato believed that we all have a daemon who is assigned to us at birth—a gender-neutral "noble spirit" who guides us on our paths and helps us make wise choices. Socrates said his daemon frequently warned him about things he should not do, but never actually told him what he should do. He called this personal guide his "internal oracle," and referred to it as a nonlocal voice or an inner nudge that encouraged him to seek the best path.

The Hellenistic Greeks taught that there were both good and bad daemons. These were similar to the *djinn* found in religions of pre-Islamic Arabia, who could be both benevolent and malevolent. These spirits probably morphed into the Christian belief in angels and demons. Most traditions described these beings as felt, but not seen. Hesiod described them as "invisible and wrapped in mist."

Pioneering psychologist Carl Jung wrote about encountering his own guide, whom he called Philemon, in a dream. This is a common way for guides to connect with us. When we dream, our defenses are down and our bodies are at rest, leaving our souls free to soar and connect with the spirit world. Our guides communicate with us through dreams, through synchronicities, and through that inner knowing we all get when our intuition speaks to us. Jung was so intrigued by this experience that he even painted a picture of his guide.

Traditional spiritualism and theosophy recognize a number of spirit guides in addition to a main guide— among them healer guides, teachers, chemists (who attune our spiritual vibrations), protectors, messengers, and gate-keepers who guard the doorway to the other side and make sure that only positive beings connect with us.

Let's take a look at some of the roles these various guides can play on your own team of allies.

Team Players

Like all of us, you have a team of allies who work to keep you on your path and following your soul plan. Some are guides—spiritually wise beings who offer to use their experience from previous lives to help you on your journey. Some are angels. Others are ancestors and loved ones who assist your guides and angels. And you may also have animal guides and other spirit guides who come and go on your team to assist you with various aspects of your life.

Working with these allies helps you remember who you are and why you are here. They inspire your creativity, your vision, and your spiritual connection. They encourage you to love yourself more fully and see yourself as the spark of the creator from which you came, enabling you to open up to more abundance in all areas of your life. They also protect you and offer incredible insights into problems and challenges.

Every one of us has at least one spirit guide and one guardian angel who are with us from our first breath to our last. Spirit guides are highly evolved souls who have lived before. Their purpose is to help you follow the map you laid out for yourself before birth and keep you on your path. In addition to these main guides, you will also work with several other helpers who join your team as you progress through life. Teacher guides come into your life when you start school. Healer guides come in to help you deal with illness. Other guides join the team to help you with romance, with your career, or with developing your talents and gifts. If you choose to become a parent, parenting guides join the team. If you have to help a parent, spouse, or partner through their last chapter on Earth, caretaker guides sign on.

In addition to these specialist guides, you also have guides I call "cheerleaders." These allies have beautiful, motivating, and uplifting energy. Their sole job is to be the "wind beneath your wings," to lift you up and help you remember to laugh when times get tough.

And then there are the protector guides, whose job is to guard and protect your energy, although they cannot protect you from learning your lessons. Let's say that you meet someone in your twenties to whom you are instantly drawn. It feels like perfect kismet. In the moment, it may feel as if you've met your soul mate. But this is often a sign that you have karma to balance with this person—perhaps someone who hurt you in a past life. It may be your karma in this life simply to be with this person and engage the hurt again, but this time to learn how to move past it. Can your guides save you from this person hurting you? No. It's your karma, your chosen path. But they can protect you by putting the right people in your path to help you navigate your way through setting boundaries and healing this karma once and for all. As you're nursing the heartache, they may help you meet a great new friend, or discover a wonderful therapist, or come upon a book that helps you heal.

Your guides communicate with you in various ways— through intuition, through synchronities, and through sensations, symbols, and images. And when it comes to understanding the messages they send you, it's all about reading these signs.

Reading the Signs

In the early stages of my development, I had a dream in which my spirit guide tried to show me what it's like to communicate with our invisible helpers. He showed me an image in which I was standing in a clearing on one side of a vast, thick forest, while he was standing in a clearing on the opposite side. He explained that every time you meditate or ask for a sign, you clear a path through this forest to the guide waiting for you on the other side. The more you solicit this interactive relationship, the more trodden and clear this path becomes. When you choose a sign for your guide and then ask to see this sign in your daily life, you validate your relationship to that guide and make the connection between you much easier.

One way to build this connetion is to ask your guides for signs by which to recognize them. Choose a sign from nature—a butterfly, a feather, or a specific animal—then ask your guide to show you this sign within a certain time frame. This is important, because your guides exist in a world outside the dimensions of time and space that constrain your world. Once you've chosen your sign and set the time frame, release your request and allow your guide to present the sign to you in a unique way.

One listener shared this experience after she asked for a sign.

I work from home, and I decided to take my dogs for a walk in an effort to reset myself emotionally. I knew it was a ridiculously specific request, but I asked my guides to show me three white feathers on my walk with the dogs. As we were heading back, I felt nudged to follow a different route. About a block from home, I stopped in disbelief. There were three white feathers, just as I pictured, placed neatly in a row in the middle of the sidewalk. I felt so loved and so heard.

What's important here is that, after asking for her specific sign, this listener followed her intuition. When she felt guided to take a different route home, she found the three feathers.

You can ask your guides to show you signs that will let you know if you're on the right path or if you're making the right decision. Another listener sent me this email about her guide assuring her through signs in nature.

After listening to your recent episode on asking for signs, I decided to give it a try. My son has been having trouble since graduation. He'd moved far away for a job and then was laid off. He wasn't sure if he should stay there and look for a new job or return home to be with family and friends and find a job here. I told him he could move back home for a bit while he got settled, but I wondered if I was doing the right thing. Was I coddling him too much? Should I encourage him to stick it out? So I asked my guides to show me a deer in the next three days if I'd made the right decision.

The next morning as I was brushing my teeth, I suddenly got an urge to have my morning coffee out on the deck. I never do this, because I'm always rushing off to work. But I'm glad I did because, as I sat there drinking my coffee, a beautiful deer walked into my backyard followed by a fawn. I knew it was my guide's way of saying: "Hang in there, Mama. You're doing the right thing for your son."

Raising Vibrations

Meditation is the best way to connect with your guides. When you meditate, you quiet your mind and push away the noise of everyday life so you can learn what your guide's "calling card" is. For example, you may smell a flower or see a certain color. You may feel a little pressure or a tingling sensation on one shoulder. When you take the time to go within, you not only reap physical and emotional benefits, you also enable your personal energetic vibration to lift and rise so you can connect with your guides.

Everything vibrates. Even objects that appear to be still are oscillating at their own frequency. And just like everything else, we each have our own personal vibratory frequency. But here on Earth, we vibrate at a much slower rate than our guides, our angels, and our loved ones on the other side. Because they are no longer encumbered by their bodies, their energy spins incredibly fast.

Let's use a ceiling fan as an example. If you were a fan, your vibratory energy would be spinning so slowly that you could see the dust on your fan blades. If your guides were fans, on the other hand, their energy would be spinning so fast that you wouldn't even be able to see the fan blades at all. When you make the time to meditate, you raise your own vibration, which greatly increases your ability to connect with your guides.

Scientific studies have proven that, when two objects vibrating at different rates come into contact, something amazing happens. The two objects start to synchronize and vibrate at the same rate. Researchers call this phenomenon "spontaneous self-organization." This means that, when you meditate with the specific intent to increase your vibration in order to connect with your guides, you come into relationship with them and they, in turn, will learn smoother ways of communicating key lessons and insights to you.

Try this simple practice. Sit in a comfortable, upright position. Breathe in and out slowly and deeply for about five minutes. Focus your attention on the base of your spine and visualize a golden ball of energy there. With each intake of breath, visualize this energy rising up and expanding along your torso, until you can imagine it spilling out the top of your head and shining like a beacon up into the sky. This golden light will protect your energy and help uplift your vibration. Ask your main guide to come stand with you, and then wait patiently while you enjoy sitting in the silence of your own energy. Pay attention to all your senses. Do you feel a presence standing by your shoulder? If you try this each morning for just five to ten minutes, you'll soon learn to recognize your guide's calling card.

Naming Guides

It is not important to know your guides' names, but it does help to establish a more personal connection with them. In his book *How to Meet and Work with Spirit Guides*, Ted Andrews writes:

> Names are not as important as the information that comes through the spirit guide. Ask your guides for names anyway, as it always helps to personalize the relationship. Trust the first name you get, even if it does not seem to fit. Many guides will give you a name that you can remember and relate to. It is not unusual for the name given not to be the true name of the guide.

This makes sense because, if your spirit guides are evolved souls who've returned to Earth many times, they've used dozens of names. Think about your own life and all the names by which you're known. I've been called Sam, Samantha, Ms. Fey, Mom, the Crystal Chick, the Psychic Teacher—and I answer to all those names.

In his book *Journey of Souls*, Michael Newton describes revelations his clients had about life on the other side while under hypnosis. Many of them couldn't verbalize their guide's name because the sound couldn't be duplicated with the human voice box. Newton believes it is much more important to understand why certain guides are assigned to you rather than learning their names. Most of his clients refer to their guides simply as "my friend."

While I agree with this, I do think it's nice to name your guides to establish a personal connection with them. You may already know your guide's name and not even realize it. Sometimes when I'm doing a reading, a client's guide shows up and I receive a name. Often, clients says: "Oh my gosh! That's the name of my imaginary friend from my childhood." One client emailed me this after a reading.

> In your reading, you said that one of my spirit guides' name is Penelope. My mom bought me a cactus when I was nine years old and, strangely enough, for some

reason, totally out of the blue, I named it Penelope. It's the only plant I have ever "named" and my family still talks about my cactus Penelope.

In another reading, I saw that a client was going through a very difficult time. The guide who showed up for her was a Japanese man dressed for battle. He said his name was Takeshi and he was protecting her energy as she went through this big transition. After the reading, she researched the name and discovered that *takeshi* is a Japanese word meaning "warrior." This made me wonder if Takeshi was her guide's actual name or a metaphor for his role on her team.

The best way to receive your guide's name is through meditation. A friend of mine told me that, years ago when she was meditating on her guide's name, she saw an image of a man writing "McCabe" on a chalkboard. She wondered if it was just her hopeful imagination— until she got to work and saw that her first patient of the day was a man named McCabe. She brushed this off as a coincidence—until her husband sent her an article he thought she'd like about a man named John McCabe who had saved his neighbor's life by administering CPR. The next night, a friend told her about a new pub opening in town named McCabe's.

If you don't hear or see your guides' names through meditation, consider giving them a name that is meaningful or symbolic for you and use this name to foster a deeper connection with them. You can use the name of a beloved pet or stuffed animal from your childhood. Or you can choose a name that symbolically represents what you need from your guide.

Working with Guides

It's very important when working with your guides to release any fears or doubts you may be feeling. Remember that you are in control of your personal energy. You have a say over who connects with you. Test the guides who come through. Ask for signs. Trust your feelings. If something doesn't feel right, reinforce your protection and disconnect from the alleged guide.

And don't rely on your guides for everything. They aren't watching over you twenty-four hours a day, seven days a week. Don't expect them to help you with everything. They are here to guide, to offer insights, and to nudge you in the right direction. They can help to instill courage and confidence in you, to motivate and inspire you, and to keep you on your path. But it is your job to recognize the guidance, check it for authenticity, and then follow it. As Ted Andrews reminds us:

> The laws of spirit are as immutable as those in the natural world. Not learning proper techniques, rushing

the opening, allowing the ego to manifest is similar to handling high voltage wires with no insulation or before the wires are fully grounded. It will ultimately short-circuit you. There are no tricks. There are no short cuts.

Often just setting an intention for the help you need can evoke a beautiful outcome. A listener recently shared a story with me that demonstrates how important it is simply to be aware of your needs and state them to yourself and to your guides.

In November, I moved to Iowa to support my partner's work, not knowing a soul there. As the months went by, I grew lonely, as my partner was frequently away on business. I find it a bit harder making friends in my fifties than when I was younger. I went to a bookstore café and sat with a coffee to write down my intentions. Top of my list: Make new friends. Next: Make progress on my writing project.

As I sipped my latté, I heard the voices of some ladies several tables over. They were discussing their current writing projects. I had stumbled upon a writers' group! I thought about approaching them, but felt shy. Then I heard them talking about their spirit guides. Bingo! Now I couldn't *not* approach them. I politely interrupted and asked if they were a writers' group, which they confirmed. I pulled out my business card to give them my contact info and they noticed that I was a shamanic practitioner. Again, they bubbled with excitement.

I had stumbled upon my new tribe seconds after writing down my intentions. The more we talked, the more I found we had in common. We agreed that this was no accident. I came home and performed a gratitude ceremony for the Universe.

The main thing we are here to do in this school called Earth is learn how to overcome our fears. Your guides can help you with this, but it's up to you to cultivate a relationship with them that allows their help to be seen, heard, recognized, and accepted.

You can do this best through meditation, inner reflection, journaling, and requesting signs and guidance. And the best question to ask your guides is this: What are the next steps I should take to further my development?

Once you've made a request for help, you have to keep your energy in a receptive and patient mode. Be open to receiving insights during those moments in your day when your mind is on autopilot. Often, you'll get your best *aha* moments when you're driving to work, doing laundry, brushing your teeth, or enjoying a morning walk. It's crucial that you learn to recognize the language of your guides in signs, synchronicities, and inspirations.

But it is just as important that you then take the initiative to act on this help.

There are several important things you can do to increase your energy so that you can create and maintain stronger connections with your guides—some physical, some mental, and some spiritual:

- Pay attention to your diet. Notice if some foods bring your energy down and if others help you feel lighter and more energized. Drink lots of water. Exercise and move your body each day. Get out in nature. Get plenty of rest.

- Monitor your thoughts and work to overcome your personal doubts and fears. Are you afraid of making a connection with the other side? Are you afraid of getting something wrong? Being led astray? Take time to examine your true inner fears. Work on relaxing your energy. Try tensing and then releasing all your muscles from your feet up to your head. Try alternate-nostril breathing. Work on increasing your visualization skills. Visualize a candle flame and see it getting brighter and brighter.

- Work on meditation, both active and passive. Try repeating a word over and over; listen to a guided meditation. Or you can simply sit in silence allowing thoughts to pop into your mind and drift on by. Do a chakra-cleansing meditation weekly. Take an intuitive-development class to learn how to work with your own energy and that of others.

All these activities can help raise your vibration so you can forge stronger links to your guides.

Finally, once you've received assistance from your guides, don't forget to thank them. I like to thank my guides by performing a random act of kindness for a stranger as an offering to them. You can donate food to a local shelter, drop off blankets or treats at an animal rescue center, or make a meal for a friend who is having a tough week. All of these actions combined will help you nurture and grow a beautiful relationship with your guides.

Requesting Help from Guides

Ask your guides to help you with small things at first so you can build up trust. You can ask them to help you find a parking space or to have a quiet, easy day. Ask them to bring you answers in your dreams. If you have a problem at work, ask them for insight. When you receive an idea, try it and see if it works. Talk over your problems with them. You may receive a flash of insight during this conversation that will help you. Sometimes you may even hear a message, as this listener did.

My husband and I were offered a position to manage a motel for two years in New Zealand, which is where he was born. Neither one of us had experience doing this, and I had lived in California my entire life. So this was a big decision for us. It meant leaving our home and good jobs. After months of debating the pros and cons, I decided to sit on my meditation pillow and ask for the answer. Before I even finished the question, I clearly heard: "Go. It will be a wonderful adventure and I will be with you, as I always have been." Although the word "adventure" was not part of my vocabulary, a warm and loving presence washed over me, and I knew that we were moving to New Zealand.

I told my husband as soon as he walked in the front door. He was somewhat surprised, because we had been leaning toward not going, especially with a global pandemic looming. But the timing of every single event for the next two years was not of this world. We never experienced the pandemic that was driving the rest of the world mad. We now find ourselves bouncing back and forth between countries with a new spirit of adventure for travel. We no longer feel bound to our house, our belongings, or our jobs, and somehow the money seems to appear to support this new lifestyle. We are in our sixties and feel as if the world is our oyster.

Clearly this listener's guides were watching over her and leading her to fulfill her soul plan.

You can also ask for assistance through signs. Choose a sign like a purple flower, a red bird, or a yellow butterfly, and ask to see it in an unusual way within a certain time frame. For example, if you're trying to decide if you should go back to school or stay at your current job, sit in meditation and ask your guides: "If I should go back to school, please show me a yellow butterfly in an unusual way before the weekend." Seeing these signs can help validate what you're seeking, and can also provide invaluable help in making decisions.

When one client was trying to decide if she should take a new job, she was excited about the offer, but afraid to uproot her family and move across the country. When she sat in meditation, she asked her guides to show her a skeleton key if she should accept the job. That night when she was watching TV, one of the actors bought a skeleton key at an antique fair, but my client brushed this off as a random coincidence. Then two days later, an artist friend stopped by with a gift—a windchime made out of skeleton keys. What are the odds? She accepted this as a positive sign and was shocked by the ease of her transition. The house sold quickly; her children loved their new school; and she received a promotion at her new job.

You can even ask your guides to help loved ones, as this story from a listener reveals.

I have a fifteen-year-old son who started high school this year and has been going through the normal trials of youth—friendship changes, girlfriends, and sports. As his mother, I was feeling useless in my ability to help him navigate all these life lessons. One day when I was feeling particularly emotional and lost, I wiped away my tears and had an emotional conversation with my guide, asking that he talk to my son's guide to help him gain the confidence he needed to succeed in his adventures. I picked some crystals that spoke to me and sat with them, giving each one some individual intentions, then I placed them on a folded piece of paper with my son's name on it.

I felt better and lighter and moved on with my day. I took a walk and asked my guide for a sign—a ladybug—to validate our connection. I am new to a lot of this and truly wasn't sure what I was doing. But I knew that I felt better.

The next morning my son got up, took a shower, and got ready for school. Right before he walked out the door, he lifted his hat to run his fingers through his hair and called out: "Mom!" When I walked over to him, I found a ladybug in his hair! We had two inches of fresh snow on the ground that morning, definitely

not ladybug weather. I cannot tell you how this validation—this ladybug in the dead of winter—has opened
my eyes, my heart, and my soul.

Be Patient

Learning to work with your guides takes time. You must
be patient with yourself and your team of invisible allies.
You are attempting to connect with beings who exist
in a different dimension. You can do this only through
focused thought, meditation, and a keen understanding
of how your personal energy field works. If you're always
thinking, moving, and going, it will be harder for you to
make this connection. If you're anxious and often filled
with worry and doubt, you must work on this aspect of
yourself first before attempting to communicate with
your guides.

If you tend to put up walls around your most difficult
emotions or often keep people at arms' length, work on
opening up your energy first before you try to connect
with your guides. These walls may be protecting you
from feeling difficult emotions, but at some point, you
must examine these defense mechanisms and ask yourself whether they are keeping bad things out or keeping
bad things in.

This is why it's so important to learn how to open to
spirit slowly and over time, through practice, patience,

and meditation. If you don't learn how to maintain focused concentration; if you don't practice meditation and learn how to properly open and close your energy; if you don't take care of your physical, mental, and spiritual self—you can create a lot of problems. You may get too much information, most of which will be wrong or from lower energies, or you may not establish any connection at all.

Finally, it's crucial to keep at the forefront of your mind the reason why you're seeking this connection with your spirit guides. You don't connect with your guides for magical gifts and psychic insight. Cultivating a relationship with them expands your consciousness, helps you understand your soul purpose, and increases your spiritual wisdom and insight.

Protect Yourself

When working with the unseen realm, it's extremely important to protect yourself and test the information coming through. There are nefarious beings out there who will try to take advantage of a novice or a person desperate for help. If you put out a call to "anyone" for assistance, "anyone" can answer you. But if you work to ground and protect your energy and set healthy, positive boundaries combined with a clear intention, you will shield yourself from negative energies. Try framing your intention in a positive way, like: "As I sit here meditating in the light and protection of love, I intend to connect with my personal spirit guide for help, insight, and healing."

There are numerous spiritual teachers who insist there is nothing negative in the world, either seen or unseen. They believe that all negativity is created in our perception. Even if that's true, however, many of us perceive a world that is filled with bad news and malevolent people waiting to take advantage of others. We live in a world of duality—a world defined by up and down, left and right, day and night. By extension, it follows that there are also positive and negative beings out there. This is why it's imperative to learn how to ground and protect your energy before attempting this inner work of connection.

Even seemingly positive beings who try to connect with you may inadvertently harm or scare you in their zealous desire to connect with the living world. Carl Jung wrote about a spirit who tried to communicate with him for help in getting his message out to the world. But Jung worried that he was being possessed or haunted by him. His oldest daughter saw a ghostly figure pass through the room. At almost the same time, his second daughter told him that, twice during the night, her blanket had been thrown to the floor. His young son began experiencing scary dreams that woke him in the middle of the night. He wrote about this experience in his memoir.

It began with a restlessness, but I did not know what it meant . . . There was an ominous atmosphere all around me. I had the strange feeling that the air was filled with ghostly entities. Then it was as if my house began to be haunted. . . . The atmosphere was thick, believe me! Then I knew that something had to happen. The whole house was filled as if there were a crowd present, crammed full of spirits. They were packed deep right up to the door, and the air was so thick it was scarcely possible to breathe.

I include this story, not to frighten you, but to demonstrate how important it is to remember that, in this other world, which is invisible to us here on Earth, there are many beings—some bad, some good, some a mixture of both.

One aspect of working as an intuitive medium that has surprised me the most is that people don't change much upon death. I always assumed that, when we died, we suddenly became enlightened and evolved—that when our souls ascended to our idea of heaven, we gained access to the mysteries of the Universe and realized the importance of love, peace, and service. But in my twenty years of doing readings and connecting with souls on the other side, I've discovered that people tend to stay the same. They may feel remorse and forgiveness as they recognize the consequences of their actions, but, until we graduate once and for all from the University of Earth, we tend to grow and evolve in inches rather than miles. This is why it's so important to test the messages you receive from your guides.

There are many ways to do this. Here are just a few questions you can ask yourself:

- Are the messages positive and uplifting? Anything that comes through that is rude or negative or judgmental is not from a higher guide.
- Does the message feel right? Trust your inner knowing. If it feels off, break the connection and reinforce your psychic boundaries.
- Does the insight received later prove true? If not, you may be working from your imagination or connecting with lower energies.
- Does the connection leave you feeling hopeful, optimistic, and filled with new ideas?
- When you ask for signs, do you receive them within a few days?

Ego vs. Intuition

One of the best ways to communicate safely with your guides is to discern the difference between your ego and your intuition. Sometimes you may believe that you're getting messages from your guides when it's really just your ego screaming at you. So how can you tell the difference?

Your ego is fear-based, so messages from it will be impatient, scary, and inconsistent. Messages from your spirit guides will be calm, loving, reassuring, and consistent. Try getting really quiet and going within. The first few thoughts that pop into your mind are usually from the ego. Pay attention to the tone, pace, and energy of these thoughts. The ego's messages will be anxious, worrisome, or fear-based. After all, its main job is to protect you, so it will use these anxious thoughts to keep you on task and safe.

If you sit in silence long enough, you will eventually hear the voice of your intuition. Notice the difference in tone. Your intuition is gentle, kind, and loving. Its messages come as a sort of knowing. You may feel it in your body first—usually in your stomach area (which is where we get the phrase "trust your gut") or in your heart center. Your guides will use your intuition to speak to you through feelings, whereas the ego always speaks in words and thoughts.

Say, for example, that you're looking for a job. You go for the interview and are offered the position. But you feel something is "off" about it. The boss is a bit shifty when you ask about the salary. The other employees seem on edge. Nonetheless, you tell yourself: "Look, I need this job. It's a great job. It will be fine." The feelings you have about something being off with the job is your intuition sending you a message. Your frantic thoughts pushing these feelings down and insisting that everything is fine is your ego trying to protect you and make sure you stay employed and are able to pay the bills. But it's your intuition that really protects you in the truest way. And keep in mind that the ego is often wrong, whereas your intuition never lies.

You can also tell it's your ego communicating if the messages you receive include a lot of information telling you why it's right and your intuition is wrong. Your intuition doesn't need to defend itself. The ego does.

The messages of the ego are often about lack and not being enough. Its messages may be warning you that you're not good enough, or that you should be working harder, doing more, or looking better. The ego reminds you to climb higher, get more, make more, and do more. It is judgmental, and its messages will often contain opinions about people around you. But it mostly loves to judge you: "You're doing that wrong." Or "You're trying too hard." Or "You're not doing enough." Or "What were you thinking when you said that?"

Moreover, thoughts and messages from the ego often change. If you've set a New Year's resolution and have already broken it, for example, one day the ego will tell you it's because you're lazy, and then it will switch to a new message, perhaps saying that you didn't have the right resources to achieve your goal. And it may switch to a new reason on the next day and the next.

The ego second-guesses everything and over-analyzes all your actions and thoughts. By contrast, when your intuition sends messages, it's your soul—your true essence—speaking. Intuitive messages are therefore loving, kind, calm, and consistent. They are typically accompanied by a physical sensation. You may feel the rightness of the message in your gut or you may experience chills or a tingling sensation. Intuition communicates in very quiet, subtle ways. Often its messages come without any emotion at all. They're just there—at the core of your being—waiting to be known.

The most important factor in connecting with your guides is to remain open to your intuition. Get in touch with the still small voice within. Pay attention to your surroundings. Listen to the music playing around you and in your head. Spend time out in nature. Record your dreams. Begin a conversation with your guides and know that you have a team of allies who are on your side, cheering you on and helping you stay on your path— even when that path is lonely, challenging, and scary. Communicating with your guides will help you feel more connected, happier, and more supported as you follow the map of your life's journey.

Light Lessons: Meeting Your Spirit Guide

This guided meditation can connect you with your spirit guide and allow you to receive the messages you need.

Start by recording yourself reading this meditation. Take your time between each sentence so that you create a slow, relaxing pace. Listen to the guided meditation each night for a week to strengthen your connection with your spirit guide.

When you feel ready, sit down in your preferred meditative position. Hold some crystals in your palms that are known to help facilitate a connection with your guide—like selenite, labradorite, kyanite, or clear quartz. Take some deep breaths to relax your energy, then state an intention for your meditation such as: "It is my intention to connect with my spirit guide." Close your eyes and do some deep breathing to bring yourself into a calm, relaxed state. Allow yourself a moment to just sit and relish the peace of your silence and solitude.

Visualize your energy opening up to the universal light of love as you take a deep breath. As you exhale, imagine all stress leaving your body. Feel the muscles in your head, neck, and shoulders release; let go of fatigue and tension. Inhale another deep breath, feeling your belly expand. As you exhale, feel your chest, back, and stomach muscles relaxing. Breathe this soothing energy into your arms, hands, and fingers. Inhale again deeply and feel your legs and feet releasing and relaxing.

Focus on your breath, feeling it expand your belly as you fill with a sense of deep peace and relaxation. Visualize roots growing out of the soles of your feet, grounding you into the Earth's healing, nurturing energy. Feel your energy pressing into the floor beneath you and going down, down, down into the Earth's core, anchoring your energy.

Starting at your root chakra at the base of your spine, see a red light begin to glow. As you inhale, see yourself breathing in this rich, red light. Visualize this red color swirling throughout your body and settling into a perfect circle of spinning energy at the base of your spine.

Move up to your sacral chakra and see an orange light glowing. Breathe in this orange light and feel it coursing through your head, neck, and chest. See it spilling into your arms, legs, and feet before it settles into a circle of spiraling orange energy below your navel. Then move your attention to your solar plexus in your stomach area. See your yellow chakra shining brightly. Breathe in this confident, joyful yellow energy and see it swirling through your body, breaking up any stagnant, old energy before it settles into a circle at your core, like your very own ball of sunlight shining out from within you.

Move to your heart center and see a glowing green light. Visualize this emerald light shining all around you and within you. As you inhale this emerald-green light, feel the sensation of pure love moving through your body, filling you with its calm, loving energy. Send the emerald-green light to any areas of your body that feel sore, tired, or stagnant, and see this energy shifting and moving fluidly throughout your whole body. Take another deep breath and see it settling into a spiraling circle of love in your heart chakra.

Shift your attention to the base of your throat and open your throat chakra. Breathe in its peaceful, sky-blue light and feel it spilling into your head, neck, chest, arms, and legs. Allow it to break up any blocks in your energy where you haven't been able to speak up for yourself, where you haven't felt heard or seen or validated. Take another deep breath and allow this serene blue light to settle into a swirling circle at the base of your throat.

Focus on your Third Eye in the center of your forehead and see its dark-blue light shining brightly. Breathe in this indigo light and feel its pulsating energy filling you as it spills into your head, neck, chest, arms, and legs. Inhale this dark-blue light and feel it dissolving any doubts or fears your energy may be holding on to before seeing it settle into a swirling circle of velvety blue light in your forehead.

Now move your attention to the top of your head. See a violet light opening, awakening, and accepting the divine into your being. Breathe this violet light through your whole body, feeling it gently burn away old blocks of loneliness and feelings of disconnection. Breathe this healing purple light into every cell of your body. Feel your tissues, muscles, and bones soaking this healing purple light into your energy. Visualize it settling into a ball of energy at your crown chakra and shining out above your head. See it shining up and spilling down all around you, like a fountain of light.

Now move your attention to a spot about a foot above your head and see a brilliant white light awakening, spinning, and shining down into your energy. Take a deep breath as you inhale this light and allow the universal light of love and protection to pour in. Feel this light flowing through your body. Breathe it into your muscles, cells, and tissues. Continue to breathe deeply as you feel more and more relaxed. You are now grounded and open. Awake and rested. Ready and relaxed.

Imagine that you are in a relaxing place like a meadow, the seaside, or a garden. Picture a sloping mountain to your right and move in that direction. As you begin climbing the mountain, keep breathing deeply. Ignite all your senses. Breathe in the fresh air. Feel the breeze brush past you. Listen to the quiet call of birds in the distance. See the beautiful vista around you as you ascend the mountain.

When you get to the top of the mountain, you find a large circle made out of quartz crystal. Stand in the middle of the circle and breathe in the energy of this mystical place. You notice a path of light illuminated before you. Send out an intention to meet your guide at the end of this path. Then follow it, knowing that the spirit guide who is working most closely with you now is waiting for you there. Be patient. Continue breathing deeply as you follow the path. As you come to the end of the clearing, take a moment to greet your spirit guide. You may see a light or just feel a presence. Pay attention to your senses. What do you hear? What do you see? What do you feel all around you?

When you're ready, ask your spirit guide if he or she has a message for you. Is there anything you should be doing? Anything on which you should focus? Are there any blocks in your path that your guide can point out to you? Take a moment to ask for information on anything you wish to know more about.

Your guide hands you a box and tells you that it holds a sign that you will see in the next week to validate this experience. It may be a sign from nature, a flower, a coin, or a photograph of a symbol. Accept this box and take a moment to study your sign.

Thank your guide for its time. As you watch your guide disappear from view, take a moment to gently close down your chakras. Visualize the purple light dimming and then the indigo light. See the sky-blue light at the base of your throat fading. Slowly extinguish the emerald-green light, then the golden yellow light. Take a deep breath and see the orange light grow dim and then the red light. Visualize your whole energy encased in light and shining brightly. Thank your spirit guide for its help and service. Take another deep, centering breath and, when you're ready, flutter your eyes open.

CHAPTER 3

Your Angel Allies

Dear Soul,

Now that you're a bit more familiar with your spirit guides, it's time to meet your guardian angel, who is with you from your first breath to your last. And you will have other beings from the angelic realm who are willing and able to assist you on specific aspects of your soul plan. Please remember that, as a student at the University of Earth, you are living under the law of free will. This means that your allies cannot intervene to help you unless you explicitly solicit their assistance through prayer, meditation, and direct requests for guidance.

One of the most challenging aspects of being a student here is that you will often feel alone. Our curriculum has been carefully designed to challenge you in these solitary times to help your soul grow in resilience and inner strength. Bear in mind that you've been accepted into the University of Earth because we know you have it within you to meet the necessary requirements for graduation as you soar to new heights. The information below should help you recognize the subtle, yet powerful, help your angelic allies can provide as your soul prepares to earn its own wings upon graduation from the school of life.

WE ALL HAVE A GUARDIAN ANGEL WHO IS WITH US always. Unfortuantely, our belief in this unseen ally is often fraught with doubt and even ridicule, so let's take a moment here to look at some of the vast historic evidence supporting a belief in these angelic beings.

Almost every major religion throughout the ages and across cultures has expressed a belief in divine messengers who are here to help us. The Greeks called them *angelos,* which means "messenger" and from which our word "angel" derives. The Hebrews called them *malakh,* which also means "messenger," and taught that we all have 11,000 of these divine beings associated with us. The Persians called them *angaros,* which means "courier."

Ancient Assyrians and Babylonians also believed in guardian angels. Zorastrians believed that we each had a *fravarti,* which was the same as a guardian angel, and ranked angels in seven main categories. Ancient Greeks wrote about daemons; ancient Romans talked about their *genius* guiding them; many different indigenous cultures teach that everyone has guardian spirits. Islam teaches that we each have four angels, or *hafaza*—two to watch over us during the day and two to guard us at night. Hindus believe in several divine messengers, among them *ghandharvas* and *asparas*, who are similar to guardian angels. Buddhists believe in *bodhisattvas*, who help in our daily prayer requests.

In all traditions, these beings are messengers of the divine. In most, they are beings that have never lived as humans, although there are exceptions. It is said that the prophet Enoch, for example, was taken up to heaven and became the angel Metatron.

There are hundreds of examples of angels at work through the centuries. They are mentioned over 300 times in the Bible, and they have been witnessed, experienced, and written about from ancient into modern times. Archangel Gabriel is said to have helped Mohammed write the Koran. Angels told Joan of Arc how to defeat France. Catholics believe everyone has a guardian angel and celebrate guardian angels each October. Saint Patrick conversed often with his own guardian angel, named Victoricus. An angel is said to have appeared to Saint Catherine, prompting the establishment of a sacred shrine in Burgundy. An angel named Moroni appeared to Joseph Smith, which led to the creation of the Church of Jesus Christ of Latter-Day Saints. In World War I, German forces suddenly backed off from a guaranteed victory while fighting the English in Belgium because they reported seeing British reinforcements arrive. In fact, the exhausted British unit was destitute and alone. Yet dozens of soldiers swore they'd witnessed luminous, winged beings appearing out of nowhere to help the English. Padre Pio—a saint who received the stigmata of Christ—said his guardian angel helped him translate the thousands of letters he received from all over the world requesting healing.

The angelic realm has been divided into a hierarchy since at least the fifth century, when Pseudo-Dionysius the Areopagite studied many ancient religious texts and began ranking angels into what he called "nine choirs": seraphim, cherubim, and thrones, who sat closest to God; dominions, virtues, and powers, who governed the Universe; and principalities, archangels, and angels, who focused on humanity and our connection to source, growth, and healing.

Angelic Signs

If the angelic realm was historically divided into a hierarchy, it makes sense that our team of invisible allies is as well. When you were in school as a child, you had a teacher helping you in the classroom every day. In addition to your classroom teacher, you probably had an art teacher, a music teacher, a gym teacher, and perhaps even after-school instructors like coaches, and dance or piano teachers. Similarly, you have a main guide as well as helper guides who assist you on your path. If we stay with our school metaphor, your guardian angel is like the principal, who oversees your soul plan and tends to intervene only when necessary. If you talk back in class, your teacher will handle it in the classroom. But if you get into an altercation or are failing a class, you're off to see the principal.

While your guides are here to help you with the intricacies of your daily life, your angel allies are here to help you with the big stuff—the dark nights of the soul, those times when you feel you're at a crossroads in life, or when you're in a disastrous situation. One of my friends used to volunteer her time teaching in a prison. She once told me of an inmate who swears he saw his guardian angel twice. When he was in the throes of a drug addiction and had decided to rob a convenience store, he awoke to a glowing light illuminating his dark room and heard an internal voice say: "Don't do it." Unfortunately, he ignored this voice and ended up in jail, where he saw his angel a second time and heard the same internal voice say: "Stay strong and faithful. You will get through this." The man recovered from his addiction, served his time, and now works as a therapist helping recovering addicts.

There are many signs that your angels are near. You may feel lighter or have an overwhelming sense of calm that doesn't fit your earlier mood. You may smell a beautiful floral scent in the air, or find feathers. You may feel a tingling sensation up your spine or down your arms, or hear a buzzing or experience a total lack of sound in one ear.

Connecting with Angels

There are many ways to contact your angelic allies for guidance. For instance, you can write them a letter. I do this every year on my birthday. This is a great way to focus and connect with the angelic realm. Get yourself into a relaxed state of mind. Try some deep breathing exercises or listen to a guided meditation. Set the scene to allow for deep connection. Choose a time when you won't be disturbed; play some calming music; light a candle or burn incense; put a few drops of lavender oil in your diffuser. Then take out your journal or some stationary and write a letter to your angels explaining any worries, fears, or challenges you're feeling. Ask them to give you insight through dreams, signs, and synchronicities, and ask for action steps you can take in order to work through any blocks you may be experiencing.

You can also thank angels in your prayers. There's an old story about a woman who was given a tour of heaven. Her guide took her to a crowded room filled with bustling angels. When she asked what happened there, she was told that this was where all the prayers for help were received and organized. Then she was led to another room crowded with angels and told it was where prayer requests for health and healing were received. They traveled from one busy room to another, all filled with angels trying to help humanity. Finally, her guide showed her an almost empty room where one lone angel sat. When she asked what happened there, her guide replied: "This is where we receive thanks for the work we do."

Unfortunately, we often forget to thank our guides and angels when we've received the help we requested. My Reiki teacher once suggested that we take time each month to send healing energy to our team of allies as a way of saying "thank you" and giving back for the hard work they do. When I take time to send Reiki energy and love to my allies, it fills me with an enormous sense of peace and gratitude. Make time each month to pause and thank your angels. Leave angel coins around as a way of giving back—at the doctor's office, in the grocery store parking lot, or in the park where you walk your dog. Or perform a random act of kindness for someone and offer it up as thanks. All of these actions help establish a strong, reciprocal link between you and your angels.

Read about angels. Have you ever noticed that, when you fall asleep reading a book, what you were reading about usually appears in your dreams? Your subconscious is very receptive at night as you prepare for sleep. What you choose to fill your mind with as you fall asleep fills your subconscious mind and primes the pump for your dreams. So when you read about angels, whether it's stories of them helping others or a work of fiction, it reminds you that help is out there and, as an added bonus, it prepares your subconscious to allow your angels to visit you in your dreams.

When you ask your angel allies for help, be alert to the messages you receive. These may arrive in the form of an insightful dream, an *aha* moment, or as synchronicities and signs. When I was working on a writing project, I was stuck on how to structure the story I was trying to tell. I prayed to my angels and guides for help. The next morning in the shower, I received a download of information, and I suddenly knew how to proceed with the project.

When my friend was trying to decide if she should go on the "trip of a lifetime" even though it meant leaving her children for a few weeks and being absent from her job at a precarious time for her company, she prayed to her angels for help making the decision. The next day when she was waiting in line at the grocery store, she overheard two women talking. One said: "Susan, sometimes you just have to choose between adventure and regret. Always choose adventure." My friend's name is Susan. She felt in that moment that her angels were talking to her. She went on the trip and had a fantastic adventure.

You can also choose a sign and ask your angels to show it to you during times when you need comfort and reassurance, as this listener's story illustrates.

I asked my angels for a sign that they were watching over me. A special sign for me has always been a red balloon. As I was driving home during a very challeng-ing time in my life, I asked my angels for help. No more than thirty seconds later, a bunch of red party balloons went right over my car. Last week, I asked for another red-balloon sign. There was nothing for two days, but on the third day my father was in the garden and shouted: "Oh look at this!" I ran outside and, floating overhead very close to our house, was a great big hot-air balloon. Guess what color it was? Red, of course! I was so grateful.

Signs like this validate your requests and let you know that your connection with your angels is "up and running."

You may have heard the saying: "Praying is talking to God; meditation is listening for a response." With all the distractions bombarding you today from your cell phone, social media sites, and streaming devices, the beauty of silence sometimes feels like an antiquated notion. Yet it's only in the purity of silence that you can go within and listen to the still, small voice of the soul. It's also where your angels can best impart ideas, inspiration, and positive energy. Practicing meditation, any kind of meditation, is good for your body, your mind, and your soul. It relaxes, calms, and centers your whole being and allows for better clarity and connection with your angels.

Guided meditations are a great way to prompt your subconscious mind to be aware of angelic presences in your life, as this story from a listener clearly shows.

I once did one of your guided meditations while sitting on the beach—the one where you ask for a sign that your guardian angels are with you. I asked that my angels leave a feather as a sign. After the meditation, I left my spot on the beach and went back home to fetch my family. When, along the way, I saw feathers here and there—one in the kitchen, a seagull feather on my path—I smiled, but knew they could be explained away. When I arrived back at the beach with my family, however, I found a huge pelican sitting next to my chair, right where I had been meditating. As we approached it, a gentleman on the beach said it was the strangest thing. That pelican had been sitting next to my chair for forty-five minutes! When we all sat down, the bird still didn't move. My kids took pictures of it and it *still* didn't budge. It stayed another forty-five minutes and then flew off. I laughed because I knew that was a sign for sure.

Crystals and Books

Incorporating angelic crystals into your meditation practice can also enhance your vibrations and increase your likelihood of connecting with the angelic realm. Crystals are gifts from the Earth. Each vibrates at its own unique rate, regardless of size. You, on the other hand, vibrate at different rates all the time. Sometimes you feel up and happy, with high vibrating energy; sometimes you feel tired or sad, with low vibrating energy. When you bring a crystal into your energy field, it helps to synchronize your vibrations with its own energy. Some of the best crystals for connecting with your angels are angelite, celestite, seraphinite, selenite, and petalite. You can hold these crystals in your palms while meditating, or use them to create a crystal grid for angelic intervention and help (see the exercise below).

Angelic Crystals

- Seraphinite is a beautiful green stone with feathery markings that can help awaken your heart to receive more love and guidance.
- Angelite, called "the stone of the angels," increases telepathy, helps reduce anxiety, and infuses the aura with peace.
- Celestite helps ignite your spiritual connection through increased dream recall and heightened meditation.
- Selenite is an almost translucent crystal that induces deep feelings of peace and tranquility while opening the crown chakra to divine connections.
- Petalite is a crystal of spiritual purification that helps dissolve blockages of doubt, fear, and worry.

When your angels want you to know something, they may place a book in your path. You may find that a book just falls off a shelf while you're at the bookstore or library. A friend may feel nudged to loan you a book that provides deeper insight into a problem you've been praying about. One listener told me that, after praying for a sign that she had a team of helpers around her, a bundle of books was left on her doorstep anonymously. Among them were *We Are Here For You*, *Angel Detox*, *The Kybalion*, *Angels of Grace*, and *You're Not Going Crazy; You're Just Waking Up*.

When I was beginning my own spiritual awakening, people kept telling me to read Helen Schucman's *A Course in Miracles*. A few weeks later, I stopped at the history section in a bookstore and was surprised to see the book sitting on the shelf marked down on sale. I grabbed it and went to the spirituality section, where I found another copy of it that wasn't on sale. I took both copies up to the register and asked the salesperson whether the book was on sale or not. She typed away on the computer and said: "No, that book isn't supposed to be on sale. That's strange. Well, it must be meant for you!" Be open to receiving your own visit from a "library angel." When you walk into a bookstore or library, ask your angels to put a book meant for you in your path.

When Your Angel Doesn't Answer

When faced with the dark nights of the soul that make you feel as if you are alone, you have to channel your inner

Winston Churchill—just keep calm and carry on. The true lessons of life aren't found in what happens to you, but rather in how *you respond* to what happens to you. When you're feeling lost and alone, you can cycle into a dark pit of despair. You can choose to blame others and even your angels and guides for leaving you alone in this hard time. You can lean on the illusory power of anger to feel brave and fearless. Or you can choose to respond with grace and inner strength, knowing and trusting that this is happening to you and for you, because it's helping you evolve into a truly enlightened being.

We all have times in our lives when we feel truly alone. These dark nights of the soul are challenging for many obvious reasons, but the lasting impacts they leave on our souls are often more difficult to see. Many emerge from a dark night of the soul with their faith in question. I believe, however, that these times of feeling bereft and alone are rich with meaning and invaluable lessons. My own dark nights of the soul have taught me that every prayer is answered. It's just that sometimes the answer is "no," or "not now," or "something better is waiting around the corner for you." I've also learned that our angels are always here with us—especially during these difficult times.

When I was diagnosed with breast cancer, my interior life went into a tailspin of fear. Before the biopsy, I prayed that the test results would show no cancer. That prayer received a strong "no" response. My husband at the time had a difficult time supporting me through this journey. I prayed that he would learn how to show up for me. That prayer also received a strong "no." But the night before my surgery, I had a beautifully vivid dream in which I was walking the beach with my guardian angel. She told me not to worry, that all would be well. I answered with my typical "Yeah, right." Then she said: "Isaiah 41:10." And I woke up.

As a cradle Catholic, I've always believed in angels, but we Catholics . . . well, we don't really read the Bible, so I had no idea what my angel was trying to tell me. Upon waking, I quickly reached for my phone and searched for Isaiah 41:10, which reads: "Do not fear, for I am with you; do not be dismayed, for I am your God. I will strengthen you and help you; I will uphold you with my righteous right hand." I knew in that moment that, for whatever reason, I was supposed to be going through this difficult time, but I was not going through it alone and all really would be well. And you know what? My angel was right. The surgery went well, and I grew stronger both physically and spiritually. And I am happier now than I've ever been.

Sometimes when you're going through difficult times that are unavoidable—like the death of a parent or a child leaving home—your angels are with you more than ever, trying to hold you in love and support. This story sent to me by a listener illustrates this perfectly.

My stepmother had been in my life since I was five years old. She was kind and gentle. She was active and healthy. Then she was diagnosed with stage-four pancreatic cancer and given just months to live. She decided that she was going to fight it to the end. She walked for miles, rode her bike on back roads, and connected with nature right up until the end. She lived a year! I was heartbroken knowing she was leaving. At the end of her time with us, I was overwhelmed and needed to find some peace, so I drove to my favorite beach on a cold, blustery, windy, rainy day.

I sat in my car and watched the waves roll in on the beach and thought about the times I had spent there with my stepmother hunting for rocks, fishing, and just talking. When I became a mom, I took my kids there too, and we hunted for what we called "wishing rocks"— rocks with a white ring on them—and heart-shaped rocks. I was thinking of this and sobbing because my stepmother would soon be gone from us, and my little ones were now in high school and would soon be leaving home. It just felt like too much and I needed to let it all out and find hope and peace.

Just when I was about cried out and feeling hopeless, there was a knock on my car window. Who in the world would be out in this weather? I put my window down and there stood an old man who said: "Hold out your hand; I have something for you." He put something warm in my hand, and I closed my fingers around it. I couldn't believe the gift he had given me—a heart-shaped rock with a white ring on it. I looked up to thank him and tell him how special it was to me, but he was gone. Without a trace. I was stunned! As I looked down at my gift again, I knew he was an angel. And I have kept that beautiful gift to remind myself that my stepmother is happy and that angels are always with us.

The Queen of Angels

Mother Mary is considered the queen of angels and mother to us all. She's a wonderful resource every one of us can call upon when we need to feel maternal, loving nurturance. My mom had a strong bond with Mother Mary—which I always found ironic, since she was the farthest thing from a maternal, loving parent. She loved us, but hid it well most of the time. She had a habit of erupting into angry tirades over the smallest things—a towel left on the bathroom floor, a bed left unmade in the morning, or trash not taken out. When she got angry at one of us, we'd get the silent treatment for weeks on end. I was scared of her throughout my childhood. Yet she instilled a deep faith and love for Mother Mary in me and for that I'll always be grateful.

When I was in the third grade, my mom was hospitalized with a terrible case of food poisoning. My dad took us to see her at the hospital one day after school. Eventually I got bored and wandered down the hallway, and somehow found myself sitting in the hospital chapel. I knelt down and prayed that my mom would get better and be home in time for Christmas. But before I rose to my feet, I paused to add: "And Mother Mary, please watch over me always and maybe, if it's not too much to ask, you can step in and be like a mother to me." I felt guilty the moment I said this impromptu prayer. My poor mother was in the hospital fighting an infection and there I was asking the queen of angels to be a stand-in mother for me. I found my dad and we said goodbye to mom and headed out to the parking lot.

Walking toward the car, I stepped on something squishy lying in the parking lot. When I stepped back and looked down, I saw a beautiful hand-knit ornament of Mother Mary dressed in her traditional blue robe and wearing a little halo over her slightly bent head. I gasped and reached down for it. I put it in my pocket quickly, because I didn't want to explain to my dad that I had just prayed to Mother Mary to provide the maternal love I was so clearly craving. Now she'd responded with this ornament as a gift or sign that she was with me. I asked my dad for a tiny tree to put in my bedroom. I strung it with lights and placed the ornament at the top of it. Ever since then, I've received many more Mother Mary miracles in my life.

This listener was inspired to reach out to Mother Mary after hearing me talk about one of these miracles.

> I recently bought a Mary icon to hang from my car's rearview mirror. I began praying each day, asking that she protect me and my fellow travelers on the road that day. I started doing this after being inspired by one of your Mary stories. Less than five minutes after saying this prayer, a car cut across several lanes in front of me as I merged onto the freeway. I heard an awful sound and saw the bumper falling off the car in front of me. Time slowed down to a crawl, like a scene from *The Matrix*. I swerved to miss the bumper and the car behind me missed it as well. It was surreal. My heart was pounding. All I could think to say was: "Thank you, Mary." At home that night, a rosary appeared on my bedroom door handle. I tear up as I write this, because I am so sincerely grateful for opening the door to so many wonderful gifts from the Universe—our guides, our angels, and so much more.

Mother Mary has appeared throughout history to offer support, warnings, and gentle guidance. She appeared to the Aztecs just before they were overwhelmed by

Columbus. She visited Saint Catherine and delivered a miraculous medal when the French were going through their revolution. She appeared in Lourdes during the Napoleonic Wars and in Wisconsin before the outbreak of the American Civil War. In Fatima, during WWI, she predicted WWII. She appeared in Portugal before the 1918 flu pandemic, in Bosnia before their civil war, and in Rwanda before the genocide. And she will appear in your life too if you seek her help and intercession.

Mother Mary's help often arrives in truly miraculous ways. You may smell a strong scent of roses, or you may receive roses. You may stumble across a set of rosary beads. When I was in college, I prayed to Mary for guidance on my career path. When I went for a walk by the university's farm later, I found rosary beads resting on a fence post. When I prayed to Mother Mary for help buying my home, we found old rosary beads buried four feet down in the ground while planting bushes in our front yard. Some report hearing heavenly music. When you open your heart to the motherly love of the queen of angels, you receive countless gifts of grace, love, and guidance.

The Archangels

In addition to your guardian angel and Mother Mary, you can also call on the archangels for help and intercession.

There are six main archangels: Michael, Raphael, Gabriel, Uriel, Remiel, and Azrael. Michael, whose name means "like God," is the angel of police officers, soldiers, and firefighters. He offers physical, emotional, and psychic protection, and is always depicted with a sword because he is known to have defeated Satan in battle. Raphael, whose name means "God heals," is the angel of healing. In Hebrew, *rapha* means "healer" or "doctor." He can help heal any ailment—physical, mental, or emotional.

Gabriel, whose name means "God is my strength," is often depicted as a female. She is a messenger and also helps creative people, especially writers and artists. She's known to help open the Third Eye. Uriel, the "Flame of God," helps clear the path in front of us so we can follow our destiny. He can help avert disasters and has been known to help with writing, intuition, and getting focused.

Remiel, whose name means "Mercy of God," appears in the Book of Enoch as the angel of hope and guidance. He guides souls to heaven and is also known as the messenger guide for psychics. Azrael, the "Light of God," is also often depicted as a female. She is called "the grief counselor" and helps people who are grieving the loss of a loved one.

Several other archangels are mentioned throughout the ages as well. These include Sandalphon, Raziel,

Raguel, Jophiel, Chamuel, Ariel, Haniel, Jeremial, and Metatron.

Light Lessons: Creating an Angelic Crystal Grid
In this exercise, you create a two-dimensional pyramid-shaped grid whose square base helps you ground your intentions, while the edges and sides face the four directions, but also converge on a single point of unity. Energy can thus travel around and diagonally across at any point.

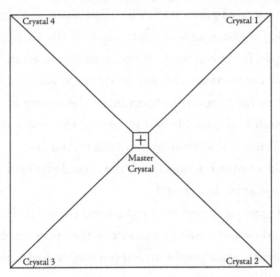

For this exercise, you'll need five crystals—a master crystal to represent your overall intent, and four supporting crystals, one for each of the four corners. You will also need one small crystal point or wand to act as your activation crystal. If you don't have a crystal point or wand, you can use your finger. In addition, you will need a small piece of note paper on which to write your intention, an eight-inch by eleven-inch (or larger) sheet of paper or square piece of fabric on which to recreate the grid pattern, and a tray or book on which to place your outline and assemble the grid if you don't have a place where it can remain undisturbed by children or pets.

Begin by replicating the grid pattern above on the larger piece of paper or fabric. Then write your intention for connecting with your angel on the small piece of paper, for example: "It is my intention to establish a deeper connection with my guardian angel." Fold the paper or fabric toward you to invite the energy of your intention into your life and place it in the center of the grid. You are now ready to build the crystal grid.

1. Cover your intention with the crystal you've chosen as your master crystal.

2. Beginning at the upper right-hand corner of the grid outline and moving clockwise to the upper left-hand corner, place your four supporting crystals, one in each corner.

3. As you do this, think of each corner crystal as supporting the master crystal in your overall intention.

4. Point your activation crystal (or finger) at the master crystal and draw an imaginary diagonal line to the crystal in the upper right-hand corner, then trace

diagonally back to the master crystal. Draw an imaginary diagonal line to the crystal in the lower right-hand corner, then trace diagonally back to the master crystal. Do the same for the crystal in the upper left-hand corner, and then for the crystal in the lower left-hand corner.

5. Finally, draw an imaginary line around the perimeter, starting and ending with the crystal in the upper right-hand corner, connecting all four supporting crystals.

6. Place your activation crystal to the right of the grid outline.

7. Meditate and/or pray before your angelic crystal grid each morning for at least three weeks to facilitate and strengthen your connection to the angelic realm.

CHAPTER 4

Your Ancestors

Dear Soul,

Now that you're familiar with your team of guides and angels, it's time to meet your team of ancestors. As you prepare for your journey on Earth, the family members who have paved the way before you are aware of your soul plan and purpose, and your life lessons. They will utilize skills they've acquired through their own earthly journeys and their innate love for you to help you fulfill your highest potential. Whether you've chosen to be raised by biological parents or adoptive caregivers, your ancestors are rooted in their love for you and your mutual goal of soul growth.

ONE AFTERNOON WHEN I WAS IN THE SECOND grade, my older sister was teasing me saying that I was adopted. She pointed out several facts to prove this: I was the only one in the family who was left-handed, the only one with curly hair, and I was born much later than my sisters. As she was joking that I had been "dropped off by gypsies" one stormy night, I was shocked and slightly appalled by the words that tumbled out of my mouth. "Thank God." I said. "That explains so much."

Spoiler alert—I was not adopted. But perhaps many of you have also had this feeling of not belonging in your family. So you can imagine my surprise when I learned that we *do* in fact choose our parents. If you think about some of the physical and emotional abuse and trauma that many experience at the hands of their parents, you must wonder: Why would anyone choose this? But when you view life through the lens of the school of Earth—a school that your soul elects to attend in order to grow— then choosing difficult parents or wonderful caregivers makes a lot more sense. Think about the story of Wayne Dyer in chapter 1. He chose his terrible father figure so he could learn and then teach self-reliance. Take a moment to think about your parents and the lessons they inadvertently and overtly taught you, and you will soon start to realize that your soul chose these experiences so it could learn, and grow, and become empowered.

Before you arrive for your first day at the University of Earth, you look over your past lives and evaluate several key questions. What have I learned? What do I still need to learn? What are my main goals for this go-round? Then your soul carefully plans out your childhood, including the struggles you need to encounter, the people you need to meet, and even the best place or environment for you to live in order to overcome your challenges and complete your goals.

Choosing Your Family

Choosing your parents is a huge, vital part of this process. It sets up all the challenges and opportunities your soul will experience as you journey through life. Let's say your soul has chosen to learn the lesson of strength. Perhaps in several past lives you had the habit of always choosing the easy way out. So in this lifetime, you choose parents who are emotionally unavailable. Perhaps after a divorce, one parent physically abandons you while the other is too busy working to care for you properly. Maybe you choose two parents who simply aren't capable of expressing love, but who can teach you that you've got to rely on your own independence and inner resources. By the end of this lifetime, you'll have learned strength.

Or let's say your soul has spent lifetimes learning the gift of healing. In this lifetime, you're ready to share that gift and teach it to others. So you choose peaceful, loving, accepting parents who are open to healing and intuition, and who will help nurture and support you. By the end of this lifetime, you will have learned how to nurture others to allow a space for healing to occur within them.

Often souls choose their parents based on a past-life experience or a family karmic connection. A grandparent may return to a grandchild as a baby because of a strong family link. If a life ended abruptly, that soul often returns to the family. After a dear friend of mine died in his twenties before completing many of his goals, I connected with him through dreams and meditation. About fifteen years after his passing, he came to me in a dream and said he was getting ready to reincarnate to his brother and sister-in-law. I called a mutual friend and shared the news with her. She was skeptical at best, pointing out that this brother had just gotten married and the couple had said they wanted to wait several years to start a family so they could save for a house. But my friend's brother announced later that month that he and his wife were expecting their first child. I wasn't very shocked when the birth announcement arrived introducing their new son, whom they had named after the older brother, my dear friend.

Some souls choose their parents based on the opportunities they can give them. I remember doing a reading for a woman in which I saw her getting pregnant soon. I saw that the soul of the unborn child had lived many lifetimes hating rich people. He had either been stuck in poverty or fighting against the wealthy in lifetime after lifetime, and it had become imbedded in his soul that rich people were greedy, bad, and awful. So his guides encouraged him to choose wealthy parents so his soul would learn that affluent people can be kind and do wonderful things with their money.

My mother and I had a very difficult relationship. I tried everything to heal and mend our broken ties. I tried to be the perfect daughter. I got excellent grades and went to a good school. I got my master's degree and established myself in a solid career. I did everything my mom asked of me. When that didn't work, I tried setting firm boundaries, sought the help of a family therapist, and tried desperately to connect with her in any way I could. None of it worked. She remained angry, volatile, and disappointed in me.

Then one night when I was in my forties, I had a powerful dream in which my mom and I were sitting at a lovely café overlooking the ocean. She held my hands—something she had never done in real life—and stared intently into my eyes before saying: "So how's this working for you, Samantha?" When I asked her what she meant, she let go of my hands and motioned around her. "This life, this life you chose, how's it working? When you asked me to incarnate as a true bitch of a mother to help your soul grow, I willingly agreed, because I love you so much. But I have to be honest. It's hard on me being this angry all the time."

Now it was my turn to squeeze her hands. "I know it's hard," I said, "but it *is* helping me. Look how strong and resilient I'm becoming. Thank you." She patted my hand and said: "Good, I'm glad." And then I woke up.

My therapist at the time said this dream was my unconscious mind trying to reconcile a lack of mother love. Certainly Freud and Jung would agree with that. But what my therapist didn't know was that I'd always had a rich dream life filled with precognitive dreams that have later come true. I knew from experience that my astral sojourns were rarely typical dreams. I believe that I did choose my mom, and I know that her lack of mother love—while painful to endure—has truly helped me to grow, not only in strength and independence, but also as a mother myself.

We also have evidence from children themselves that we choose our parents. Countless parents recall their children telling them how and why they were chosen. If you're a parent, you may have heard this from your own child. When my oldest daughter was three years old, she was sitting on my lap as I read her a book. She sighed happily and rested her head on my shoulder and said: "Mommy I'm so happy I picked you." My middle daughter told me I was the best mommy she'd ever had. But my youngest daughter was more specific. When she was in preschool, she had a habit of handing me a notebook and saying: "Write this down." Then she dictated stories, songs, and seriously esoteric thoughts that popped into her head. On her fourth birthday, she said: "Mom,

I'm not really four. I'm ageless. We all are." So when she climbed into my bed one night and asked if I wanted to know how she chose me, I was all ears. She said: "I remember being high up in a tower looking down at a bunch of clouds. God walked in and told me it was time to choose my parents. Then he moved his hands and the clouds went away. I saw three parents, and I pointed to you."

Sometimes children choose their parents decades before they return to this school called Earth. I received this intriguing email from a listener who believes her daughter appeared to her as an imaginary friend when she was a child.

One evening while getting my four-year-old daughter ready for bed, she stood up and said: "Mama do you remember me?" I was puzzled and told her that of course I remembered her and always would. She replied: "No Mama, do you remember me from when you were little and you lived with Nana and Dad?" I said I did. "Remember I came to play with you," she continued, "and we played hide and seek and you hid on the side of that long cabinet thing." She described herself wearing her hair in two braids tied with red ribbons and said God had told her she couldn't play with me anymore because I was getting too big. So she had to go away.

But when I was going to have a baby, she told God that she wanted to be my baby. And God said: "Yes you'll be good for her." With her beautiful little index finger, she touched my belly and said: "And bloop, he put me in your tummy! Now do you remember me, Mama?" With tears in my eyes, I answered: "Yes, Honey! Yes, I remember you!"

We said goodnight. I kissed her and blessed her and walked out of her room in tears. It all came back to me in a flood of memories. I remembered playing with my little imaginary friend with two braids. My mom told me there was no one there, but my nana told me she saw her too. When my daughter was born, I told my husband that she looked so familiar to me, as if I had known her before, but I didn't know how.

Before children are born, they often announce their presence to their future siblings, as this listener's story shows.

A few months ago, my daughter's kindergarten teacher asked me if my daughter had any siblings. When I told her she was our only child, the teacher said: "I thought so. I hate to pry, but will she be getting one? Your daughter has been drawing herself with 'her little sister' quite a bit." I was open with the teacher about how I haven't been gifted in the fertility department. I joked with her that, if my daughter kept drawing a sibling enough, she might manifest one. Well, I think she was on to something. I still can't believe it, but my husband and I are finally expecting our second daughter.

These stories all demonstrate that the makeup of your family dynamic is carefully chosen by your soul before you come to Earth.

Identifying Your Ancestors

Our family members help us learn about love, boundaries, relationships, grief, and emotional growth. And death does not sever that bond. Our ancestors are alive and existing in a different dimension, and stories and experiences from around the world show us that they are still very much a part of our lives and can see what we're going through. Moreover, they can intervene to help or offer support and sustenance during difficult times.

Your ancestors are all the people connected to you by blood relations and love. I want to stress this bond of love. The link between you and your ancestors is always based on love, not necessarily on biology. And this includes stepparents and stepgrandparents as well. If you were adopted, your ancestors include family connected to your adopted family. This comes up all the time in readings. Once when I was connecting a client to her grandmother, she interrupted me to say she was

adopted and asked if I was connecting her to her biological grandmother or her adopted grandmother. My client
was Korean, but the grandmother I was seeing appeared
to be a little Italian lady who had a fierce love for the
woman sitting before me. But then I saw two Korean
women who turned out to be her mom and grandmother, and they wanted to let her know that the family
had searched for her for years. Now, from the other side,
they were watching over her, along with her adopted
grandmother.

The ancestors who watch over you can be people
you've never met or even heard about. When my youngest daughter was born, she slept in a bassinet by our bed.
One evening, I awoke and saw a little man leaning over
the bassinet gently stroking her forehead while singing
a song in Gaelic. Startled, I sat up, but the man simply
turned to me and made a shushing motion with his finger and then disappeared. For years, I wondered who
that man could have been. Years later when we were
going through old family photos, I was shocked to see a
black-and-white photo of my father-in-law as a little boy
standing next to the man I'd seen singing over my daughter's bassinet. He was her great-grandfather. It filled me
with a sense of awe and wonder to think that an ancestor
that far back in the generational line took time to pop in
and visit the newest arrival to his family.

You can call upon your ancestors for help in any area of your life. If you have ancestors who were strong, or smart, or talented, you can ask them for help in those areas of your life. My dad often told the story of his grandmother who left Ireland with her four children for a better life in America. The day they were leaving to get on the boat, my great-grandfather said he'd meet them there and stopped at the pub for one last drink with friends. He never arrived at the boat.

I often think of my great-grandmother standing on that ship alone with four small children. She could have gotten off the boat and returned to her life in Ireland. She could have sold her tickets and moved in with her parents in Wales. But she didn't. She stayed on that ship alone and persevered through Ellis Island. I hope she found comfort when she saw Lady Liberty holding the flame of hope high. She eventually found work in a candy store. My grandfather, who was then just twelve years old, never finished school, choosing to work and help support the family instead. He started out running errands for an insurance company and retired as a vice-president of that company years later. My great-grandmother eventually owned her own candy store and raised her children by herself.

When I was going through my divorce and feeling scared, alone, and unsure, I often called upon this great-grandmother for strength. One morning when I was meditating, I asked her to give me a sign that she really was supporting me and helping me through this process. A friend popped by later that afternoon with a box of chocolates. I knew it was my great-grandmother's way of telling me that she was surrounding me with strength and that all would be well.

It often helps to ask for confirmation of your ancestors' presence around you. You can ask for a specific sign to receive validation that your loved ones are indeed with you, as this listener recounts.

I've heard you suggest that you can ask family members in heaven to show you their names in an unusual manner as a sign from them. So I asked my father to show me his name. I never knew him. My parents divorced when I was very little, and he died before I could grow up and find him again. He had a pretty unusual name—Lonnie. When I got home, I decided to sit down and watch a movie. In one of the first scenes, a character introduced herself as Lonnie. I was stunned. I don't think it had even been fifteen minutes since I had asked for a sign. I had to rewind the movie and replay it to make sure I had heard correctly. It's amazing to think that my request for a sign was answered so quickly.

Receiving signs like this from your ancestors is both comforting and validating, not only for you, but for all your family members. This listener confirmed this.

I asked my grandmother to give me a sign that she was still with us. The sign I chose was dimes. That week as we were leaving to return from a camping trip, the elderly man from the lot next to us walked over and dropped a shiny new dime into my hand. "I found this on your lot," he said. My world paused for me for a second or two. That was my sign from Grandma. I thought about how strange it was that this man should go to the trouble to give me a dime just because he'd found it on my lot. I was grateful and in awe for a minute, and then started to rationalize and question what had happened as the days went by.

So I asked my grandma if she could send me another dime. My mother-in-law dropped by the next day and, as she walked up the driveway, she bent over and picked something up. Then she walked over to me and said: "I found this in your driveway." And she placed a shiny new dime in my hand.

I was beyond delighted and decided I needed tell my mom and sisters about the experience. It would give them comfort to know that Grandma is around us and watching over us. It was a risk, because my family is very religious and, ironically, that sometimes tends to make them less open to these types of spiritual happenings. I was nervous about telling them. But they were all accepting about it and genuinely believed the dimes were from Grandma. That in itself was one of the best gifts.

Sometimes when we ask for a sign from loved ones in heaven, they go the extra step, as this inspiring story demonstrates.

Recently, I asked my mom in heaven to show me a butterfly. It was early one morning in the summer, still dark out, and I got up to let the dog out. As soon as I opened the door, I saw a monarch butterfly directly in front of me perched right on the screen. I didn't put two and two together at the time and thought it was just a fluke.

When I let the dog out, he also noticed the butterfly and started to chase it. But it kept landing back on the screen in front of me. I thought it was very strange, especially since it was still dark out, but I blew it off until later that day. I'm a nurse and was at work getting ready to discharge a patient. This patient, who had called me by my own name all day, called me Katherine. Katherine is my mom's name! Never in my life has anyone mistaken my name for Katherine. At that point, I knew the butterfly and this person calling me Katherine were signs from my mom.

It's also important to keep in mind that your ancestors can't stop a life lesson from happening, but they can help by giving you warnings or reassurance that all will be okay in the end.

Before I was diagnosed with breast cancer, I always knew that my former mother-in-law was watching over me from heaven. The night before I discovered the lump in my breast, I had a dream in which she came to me and kept repeating: "It doesn't matter, Samantha. You're going to be fine. Do you hear me? You're going to be fine." At the time, I didn't know what the dream meant, but when I found the lump the next evening, I knew what she was trying to tell me.

Soon after I'd undergone surgery, I was at my daughter's school for her kindergarten graduation ceremony. A family friend who was very close to my mother-in-law approached me and said: "Samantha, are you okay? I've been having the strangest dreams about you." I told her about my recent health issues and she said: "Oh my gosh. I should have told you sooner. I keep having these dreams where Maggie is shouting at me to tell you that you're going to be okay. It's all going to be okay."

This experience taught me that my breast cancer was meant to happen in my life. It awakened me to numerous changes that had to be made within me and my life as a whole. But it also taught me that, throughout my health journey, I was never alone. I think people often start to lose faith or hope in a higher power and an afterlife when they're going through a challenging time, pray for it to be healed or ended, and then give up hope when that prayer isn't answered. Yet, I don't think life is supposed to work that way. Our team of guides, angels, and ancestors aren't there to serve by helping us win the lottery or curing cancer. Rather they're here to offer support and comfort while we're going through difficult times.

Breaking Generational Patterns

Ancestors often to return to Earth in order to break generational patterns. When I was doing readings full time, many deceased loved ones came through with a message of apology for the way they had treated their children, whether through addiction, abandonment, or abuse. These souls had become aware of the damage they'd wrought and wanted to make amends. Most of my clients were happy to receive this apology, but some weren't ready. And I want to stress that that's okay too.

Society makes us believe that forgiveness should be our ultimate goal. I'm not sure that's always true. We can't forgive until we recognize the damage that was done to us and work to heal that first. This is how generational patterns get repeated throughout families. When we push down the reality of what we endured as children without fully accepting and feeling the pain, many unconsciously repeat this same pattern. But in my work connecting people with their guides and loved ones on the other side, I constantly hear that some are returning specifically to break these patterns. This may be why we've seen an uptick in children born with enhanced intuition and a beautiful connection to their souls.

When I was a teacher, many of my students were the first in their families to attend college. I told them that my dad and his brother had been the first in all the generations of their family to go to college. That broke a pattern in our family. For my cousins, my sisters, and myself, going to college was simply expected of us. The same is true for the emotional issues that many families deal with. For instance, when those who come from families plagued by addiction choose another path, they help break that pattern in their generational line.

I had a powerful reading experience with a client whose mom and brother came through. Both had chosen to end their lives. In fact, I later learned that at least one person in each generation of her family had chosen suicide, going back as far as anyone could remember. My client struggled with depression herself, but had chosen therapy, anti-depressants, and deep, powerful inner work, which she then taught to her own children. When her mom and brother came through in the reading, they thanked her for breaking this generational pattern.

Think about a negative pattern that's been repeating in your family. It could be anger, addiction, abuse, abandonment, issues with money, business failures, sibling problems, or love. If you're dealing with one of these issues that's been passed down to you, perhaps one of your main missions in this lifetime is to heal it so that future generations won't have to experience it. The first step to healing these generational patterns is to recognize them. Then you have to do the hard but fulfilling work of healing them before you can finally release them with love, surrender, and acceptance. "If you bring forth what is within you, what you bring forth will save you," Jesus tells us in the Gospel of Thomas. "If you do not bring forth what is within you, what you do not bring forth will destroy you."

In addition to self-help books, meditation, journaling, and prayer, you can also call upon your ancestors for help with these healing steps on your journey. Perhaps you're the person your family has been waiting for to help heal their generational patterns.

Connecting with Ancestors

In my years of doing readings, one message that consistently comes through from loved ones in heaven is:

"Thank you for remembering me." Across the globe, there are many rituals for remembering ancestors. Celtic traditions celebrate Samhain, setting an extra place at the table for departed loved ones. Latin Americans and Mexicans honor their loved ones with Day of the Dead celebrations. In China, the Qingming Festival honors the dear departed and a Chinese proverb tells us: "To forget one's ancestors is to be a brook without a source, a tree without a root." Throughout Asia, food and wine are offered to deceased family members. Hindus honor their ancestors during *Pitri Paksha*, which means "fortnight of ancestors." In Cambodia, the dead going back seven generations are celebrated with offerings of prayers. In Vietnam, they burn incense and cook the favorite foods of deceased family members on the anniversary of their death. Catholics celebrate All Soul's Day to honor loved ones on the other side.

One of the best ways you can connect with those who've gone before you is simply to remember them. Continue to celebrate their birthdays. Tell their stories. Keep pictures of them around your home. Ask your living family members to tell stories and write down details they remember about them. Do some research on the internet.

When I was in college, I took a fascinating course called History of Family. We often took field trips to historic cemeteries, where the professor taught us the

meaning of certain trees or flowers carved on grave-
stones. For our final project, we had to research one
family member thoroughly, finding as many histori-
cal records as possible. This was back when computers
were fairly new, so I trundled off to the university library
and begged the librarian for help. I was researching my
maternal grandfather. All I knew was that he had been
a stone mason from a small village outside of Milan in
Italy. The librarian walked me to a section filled with
rows and rows of green books—the records of all the
people who had come through Ellis Island. Then she
walked away.

I knew my grandfather had arrived in America around
1905, so I pulled out the book labeled "Italy—1905." I
sat down at a table expecting to spend the next several
hours looking for one name in this giant book, so you
can imagine my surprise when I flipped the book open
to the middle and my eyes landed right on my great-
grandfather's entry. It felt like a miracle. But it was also
incredibly impactful to read the name of the ship he'd
arrived on, the village he'd come from, and those with
whom he'd arrived. I even got to see a copy of his signa-
ture. Connecting with your ancestors in this way keeps
them alive for you, and I expect for them as well.

You can also celebrate ancestors in ways they'd appreciate. I have a friend who walked away from her religious heritage, but she still visits her local synagogue on

each of her parents' birthdays as a way of honoring and connecting with them. Because my father passed from Alzheimer's, I donate to the Alzheimer's Association on the anniversary of his passing. You can also make their favorite meals or desserts on their birthdays as a way of celebrating their lives. You can continue their traditions and pass them on to your own family. My mom made stuffed cabbage for Easter every year. We had the traditional ham, but it was always served with her famous stuffed cabbage. Now that she is gone, I plan on continuing this tradition with my daughters.

Asking Ancestors for Help

I learn a lot of fascinating aspects of life on the other side from doing readings. One thing that surprised me the most is that the departed have jobs in heaven. In one of my first readings, I told my client that her mother was working with babies getting ready to be born. She told me that made sense, because her mother had owned a daycare and loved children. After that reading, I started asking loved ones in spirit what they did on the other side. Musicians, writers, and painters tended to work with artists here on Earth, helping to inspire their creativity. Doctors, nurses, and therapists often worked helping newly arrived souls acclimate to their new surroundings. People who died from addiction issues worked with people on Earth to help them overcome these same problems.

One day, a woman came to see me about a romantic issue she was having with her boyfriend. She told me she did not want a mediumship reading; she just wanted intuitive information about her relationship. Nevertheless, when I connected with her energy, a man in his forties appeared in my mind's eye. When I passed on some validating information, the woman said: "Oh that's my uncle. But I barely knew him. Can we just focus on my question?"

I tried to do as she requested, but the man in spirit was insistent. He kept showing me a house in flames and repeating: "I saved them. That's my job. I'm the family protector." I asked the young woman if her family had ever been involved with a house fire. She told me that, several years ago, they had all awakened in the middle of the night at the same time to discover that the kitchen was on fire. The fire quickly grew out of control, but, thankfully, they were all unhurt. I explained that her uncle had helped to awaken them and made sure the fire department got there. "Well that is weird," she said, "because we lived way out in the country. No one could ever find our house."

Since that experience, I've learned that every family has at least one ancestor on the other side whose job is to watch over family members. You may already have an idea of who this person is in your family. Typically, it's someone who was always invested in traditions and family stories, and keeping the family connected. I had a client who inherited his grandfather's construction business. Each time he came to see me, the grandfather let him know which employees were loyal and which ones he needed to watch more closely. When the father of a friend of mine died, he came through in a reading and showed me that he had one foot in this world and one foot in the other. "I am not fully crossing over until I know everyone in my family is okay," he said. "I'll wait for my wife."

And he's been true to his word. A few months later, his wife had a dream that her husband was shouting at her to be careful driving. The next day, she cautiously drove to work and was shocked when a truck ran a red light, narrowly missing her car. "If I hadn't been so alert that morning because of the dream," she marveled, "I don't know what would have happened to me." When this man's granddaughter was wait-listed for the college she wanted to attend, she asked him for help. Two weeks later, she got a letter from the college telling her that she was admitted to the school.

Children on the other side tend to stay very close to their parents here on Earth, but even they often have jobs to do. When I was connecting a mother to her daughter, the daughter in heaven said: "I'm helping my mom and dad do something great with the pool friends." The mother had no idea what that meant, until a few weeks later when new neighbors moved in next door. The new neighbor came over and asked to look at my client's pool, because they were thinking of putting one in their backyard. The two women chatted over coffee outside by the pool and learned that they shared a terrible bond—both had lost children, one a son and one a daughter. They started talking about the lack of resources in town for grieving parents and soon brainstormed an idea to create a support group. I have no doubt that my client's daughter and her neighbor's son helped these two women meet and work together to heal their grief.

Recognizing that our loved ones on the other side are continuing their work, just in a different dimension, is incredibly helpful to healing grief, as demonstrated by this listener's story.

Many years ago, I lost my younger sister in a car accident. Needless to say, our entire family was devastated. About a month after her death, I had a dream that I met her. I ran up to her excitedly and asked how she was doing. She said she was okay, but she felt a bit unsure because she had a new job and was not sure she could do it. She said she had to help the bottled-water people. Their daughter was dying, and they did not know how to let her go. I told her she would do fine. We embraced, and I woke up.

As I looked at the clock next to my bed, I realized that I was going to be late for church. I considered not going, but, for some reason, I felt I had to get up and go. When I got to church, I sat in the parking lot thinking about how much I hate to walk in once the sermon has started. But again, I felt I had to go in. As I walked in and sat down, the minister said that he felt compelled to tell a story. Yesterday, he said, a man who was visibly upset had come into the church office. When he asked what the trouble was, the man said his daughter was dying of cancer, and he did not know how to let her go. What was the man doing at the church office? Delivering bottled water.

Because of this dream, I do not wonder if there is more than this life; I know there is.

These stories remind us that our loved ones are ready, willing, and able to help us and others when needed. All we have to do is ask for their help.

Often this help comes as wonderful validation and confirmation. When my mother was dying in the hospital, we were trying to get her transferred to a hospice center, but were told there were no available beds. Finally, we insisted on speaking to a hospice social worker. I sent up a request to my dad asking him to help us, so that mom could die with peace and dignity. Less than an hour later, the social worker came rushing into my mom's room exclaiming: "I'm sorry to keep you waiting. I was with another patient—a nice old man named Mr. Owen." My sister and I looked at each other and smiled.

My dad's name was Mr. Owen. The social worker clicked away at her laptop and said: "Well, will you look at that? A bed just opened up."

Because we live here under the law of free will, we must be the ones to ask for assistance. We must give our ancestors permission to help us, and then trust that they will. Once they do, it's important to honor them by showing gratitude or making an offering, like a donation to a charity connected to their life and interests.

If you're hoping to heal a generational issue in your family line, or if you want to call upon one ancestor for specific help and guidance, you can create an ancestor altar to serve as a visual symbol of what you're hoping to honor, create, heal, or manifest. Altars help to focus your intention and, since all the work you do that substantially effects change occurs at the subconscious level, they can become an important part of your practice.

Light Lessons: Creating an Ancestor Altar

In this exercise, you will create an ancestor altar that can help you engage, at the subconscious level, with your ancestors. Until you feel, at this deeper level, that you have healed an issue or have done the work to manifest a goal, change will not occur. By incorporating visual representations of your goals and intentions into an ancestor altar, you remind your subconscious of the change you're working to make in your life and communicate that intention to your ancestors.

First, choose a space for your altar—preferably not in your bedroom, but rather in a communal space like the kitchen, living room, or dining room. If you're new to this or living with family members who may question your need for an altar, you can always use a closet. When I began my own spiritual awakening, my family was so confused about my new beliefs and interests that I created my first altar and meditation space in my closet.

Write down your intention for the altar—for instance: "It is my intention to heal the generational karmic influence of addiction in my family line." Or "It is my intention to call upon the strength, humor, and resiliency of my grandfather." Or "It is my intention to heal generations of money issues by accepting abundance in all directions of time in positive ways now."

Choose objects for your altar that represent your ancestors. You can print a map of their country of origin to serve as a base for your altar and decorate it with objects that represent their interests. For instance, if your ancestors are from Russia, use Russian nesting dolls; if they are from Guatemala, include some worry dolls. If you have a scarf, handkerchief, or knitted shawl that belonged to them, use this, or a candle holder or piece of jewelry that represents them. You can also include a photograph of your loved ones or simply write down their full names. Then write your intention below this.

When you set up your altar, consider the four directions and the elements. An ancestor altar typically incorporates the elements of earth, fire, air, and water. In the north, which is connected to earth, place a crystal, a piece of jewelry, or a flower that reminds you of your ancestor. In the east, which is connected to air, place an incense diffuser or essential oil. Consider using a scent that reminds you of your loved one, like rose or lavender. In the south, which is connected to fire, place a candle to help light your way to the answers you seek. In the west, which is connected to water, place some blessed or holy water. You can also use a seashell here or a river rock.

In the center of the altar, place a photograph of your ancestor or simply write your loved one's name on a piece of paper. Place your written intention over this. Take a moment to center your thoughts and visualize sending them to your ancestors.

Each day, light the candle, while calling upon your ancestors for help and guidance. Pay attention to ideas that pop into your head throughout this process. If you dream at night, write down any dreams you have upon waking. They may be messages from your ancestors.

It's a good idea to create this altar at the beginning of the month or at the New Moon and keep it up for at least one month.

PART II

The School of Life

———————

CHAPTER 5

Discovering Your Soul Purpose

Dear Soul,

Great job! You've chosen your unique team of allies and have selected the primary members of your family. Now for the really fun part. It's time to decide what you want to do with your time at the University of Earth. What do you want to teach, share, or build? How will your unique perspective and talents best be used during your time on Earth?

Once you've chosen your soul purpose, you and your team will place "signposts" into your soul plan to help your heart remember what you're here to do while on Earth. These signposts can include synchronicities, meeting mentors, and receiving messages in dreams. Even if you deviate from your soul plan while attending the University of Earth, you will always find a way to express your true talents and gifts.

Never fear, dear soul. You are always on the right path.

WHEN I WAS STRUGGLING IN HIGH SCHOOL WITH choosing a college, I complained to my teacher that I had no idea what I wanted to do with my life. She patted my shoulder and said: "Go within and ask your heart. God has placed a desire in your heart for a reason. Your job is simply to identify what that is." I thanked her, but sighed inwardly. At the time, my only desires were going out with friends, seeing my boyfriend, and reading.

But when I got home and started to write in my journal about what she had told me, I realized that I had a lot of passions. I'd been writing for as long as I could remember. I liked to paint, even though I wasn't very good at it. And I loved books—all kinds of books, but especially spooky ones about unsolved mysteries and hauntings. When my mom caught me reading instead of doing one of my chores, she told me that, if I could only make a living by reading, I'd be a millionaire.

Soon after this, I discovered Joseph Campbell and his work on the hero's journey. I read how he'd spent time after college living in a ramshackle cabin in the woods just so he could read. This sabbatical led him to reformulate the way we look at the power of myths and prompted him to coin the term "follow your bliss." His writings made me wonder what my life would look like if I followed my bliss.

Shedding Labels

Life can be tricky because we all have expectations and hopes placed on us by ourselves, by our families, and by society. The weight of these can leave us feeling as if we have no choice but to get up each morning, clock into work to pay the bills, and then go home and do it all again the next day. When I eventually settled on a career that would support my passion for reading and writing, I attended a teaching conference where we had to fill out a form to introduce ourselves to the group. The form had an image of a sun in the center with several rays; the caption read: "Who Are You?" The presenter told us to fill in the sun's rays with words that described us and then share our answers with the group.

I quickly filled in my rays with descriptive terms like teacher, wife, mother, daughter, sister, friend. But when the presenter came to our table to check our progress, she looked at my paper and shook her head. "No, this isn't who you are," she said. When I protested, she took off her glasses and looked directly at me. "These are your labels," she told me. Then she ripped up my paper and suggested that I try again. This time, after some reflection, I wrote down words like book-lover, seeker, writer, spiritual, hardworking, and impatient. This exercise made me think about who I am *beneath* the labels I'd given myself. Try it yourself and see what you learn.

Write your name in the center of the sun and fill out the rays with words that describe your authentic self.

To discover who you really are beneath all the labels— your soul purpose—start by examining your passions and interests as a child. What were your favorite books? TV shows? Video games? Who were your heroes? What were your hobbies? Then look at areas in your life today where you lose track of time. What do you do that feels so wonderful and fulfilling that you forget to look at the clock? What do you want to make time for in your busy day?

As I was talking to a friend about a book I was enjoying, she said: "I don't know where you find the time to read. I never have a moment to sit down with a good book." Then she went on to describe an elaborate gourmet dinner she'd prepared for her family over the weekend. I asked her where she found the time to plan and cook such an amazing meal. And it suddenly dawned on me that I make time to read because learning and teaching are a part of my soul purpose, just as my friend makes time to cook because it's how she connects with her soul purpose, which is to care for and nurture those around her.

Love and Fear

People often believe their soul purpose must be something big like writing a best-selling novel, inventing a new product, becoming a CEO, or starting a successful business. But this is simply not true. If it were, we'd all be famous billionaires. In fact, our overall soul purpose is to learn how to choose love over fear. It's really that simple. We're here to learn how to embrace love in ourselves and then see this love reflected in everyone and everything around us. This is deceptively simple, however. To truly understand what this means, we have to understand the many layers of love and the hidden ways fear often masquerades as love.

Seeing love in others doesn't mean that you have to love those who have harmed you. It's about understanding from a place of love why they made those choices and then loving yourself enough to walk away from the situation. Nor does loving yourself mean that you have to love a terrible mistake you made. It's about lovingly accepting the mistakes you've made and learning from them in order to avoid repeating them.

When you move through life from a place of fear, you can only see love where you wish to see it. In reality, this is analogous to the wizard in the Land of Oz, who hid behind a curtain of illusions. Fear can make you hold on to anger out of a need for empowerment. It encourages you to stay stuck to avoid change. It lures you into refusing opportunities in order to feel safe and secure. Fear causes you to make terrible choices. Its siren call often pushes you off your destined path.

Choosing Your Soul Purpose

A soul often needs many lifetimes to learn how to truly love and be loved. It can take centuries of success and failure to finally kick fear to the curb. In your many journeys back to the University of Earth on your quest to embrace love and overcome fear, you may choose different soul purposes to help you learn all the multifaceted aspects of love and fear.

When I do readings, I'm often able to discern glimpses of clients' soul plans that include their soul purposes, their life lessons, and their challenges. Over years of doing this, I have become aware of several recurring themes that appear in these readings as specific soul purposes. Below is a list of those that appeared most often. See if any of them resonate with you.

- *Healer:* Healers use whatever they have learned in this lifetime and in prior incarnations to help heal others. They may be traditional healers, or they may feel drawn to intuitive work, Reiki, yoga, massage therapy, acupuncture, or aromatherapy. They may work in mainstream medicine, chiropractic, homeopathy, art therapy, hypnotherapy, herbal work, animal healing, or healing touch. Or they may work as teachers, counselors, or artists—any role that helps others connect to source energy.

- *Cycle-breaker:* Cycle-breakers may be here to heal family karma or break a recurring pattern in their family line. They may be working to break a chain of negativity that involves financial issues, or emotional or physical abandonment, or addiction, or anger. However difficult this may feel at times, it is something their souls agreed to do in order to help their family members develop their spirituality. If you are a cycle-breaker, you may have spent several lifetimes balancing out generational issues, perhaps working on forgiveness with one family member. You may serve as a teacher for your family, which can mean you feel like "the different one." This is hard work, but it is incredibly important work. By resolving negative patterns, you send healing into the past and also to future generations.

- *Creator:* Creators use their abilities to make the world a more beautiful place—both in their personal and professional lives. They may be painters, writers, chefs, knitters, writers, dancers, musicians, gardeners. They use their creativity to express love and connection, and to inspire others to see their world in a new light. Creators link others to source energy and remind them where they come from. They show others that we are all connected, that life is beautiful, and that there is always hope. Their work brings healing, confirmation, connection, and love to others.

- *Intuitive:* Intuitives tune in to and read other people's energy to help guide them on their journey. They help others return to their chosen paths when they have strayed. If you are an intuitive, you may choose to be an actual intuitive reader, or you may use this gift to help those you encounter. Family, friends, coworkers, neighbors, and strangers may feel comfortable coming to you for advice and counseling. Others may "confess" to you and feel comfortable sharing their problems with you. Because of this, you may sometimes need time alone to recharge your emotional batteries. Intuitives are sometimes described as "old souls," because they help others validate their problems and use their intuition to help them see new avenues for growth.

- *Motivator:* Motivators inspire others to be, do, think, and act their best. Their energy is so positive and uplifting that others feel better just being around them, and they are always able to find solutions to problems. Their energy is transformative, and they help others see opportunities for growth and development, encouraging them to realize who they can be and who they really are inside. If this is your soul purpose, you may work to encourage friends and family, or you may work as a coach, a motivational speaker, a counselor, or a healer. You may also excel at self-help, writing, sales, marketing, and public relations.

- *Leader:* Leaders bring out the best in others. They have the ability to see a problem and be the solution. If you are a leader, you are here to develop the humility and ethics that great leaders require and then help others do the same. You tend do the right thing even when it's not popular. You don't see those around you as competitors, but rather as collaborators. You have a clear vision for your life, and cultivate relationships with those who can help make that vision a reality. This soul purpose carries great responsibility and can be isolating, because leaders often forget to ask for help. Once they step into their light and power more fully, however, this isolating feeling melts away and they share their inner wisdom and innovative ideas with those around them.

- *Advocate:* Advocates are here to help others find their voice. They use their own experiences and empathic heart to validate others' pain and worries and help them feel connected to something greater. If this is your soul purpose, you may be involved in politics or the law, or you may volunteer to help those who don't have a voice. You may advocate for animals, for children, for the poor, or for the disenfranchised. You may work to change laws, amend bills, or educate others on matters important to them. You may be an advocate for friends and family, or you may be called to use your passion, sense of justice, and compassionate heart to create change and facilitate powerful opportunities for others.

- *Caretaker:* Caretakers are here to nurture others and make them feel safe and loved. This soul purpose may manifest as taking care of children, pets, elderly parents, or friends. This is the greatest form of healing, but sometimes caretakers resist their purpose because it can be difficult to feel as if they are here only to take care of others. But when they embrace their purpose and establish healthy boundaries and self-care, they can gain beautiful insights.

- *Teacher:* Teachers have a gift for breaking down complex subjects so others can understand them, but they're also able to use their knowledge to encourage others to dig deeper and find the value in always seeking more wisdom. Those with this soul purpose tend to be approachable, inquisitive, smart, and kind. They are passionate about learning and are true seekers of knowledge. Teachers are very adaptable and can learn how to roll with the punches. Whenever life throws them a curveball, they first study the pitch and learn how to make it work for them. Then they help others deal with their own curveballs. If this is your soul purpose, your mission on Earth is to teach others that they are capable of accomplishing amazing goals and manifesting wonderful dreams.

- *Pathmaker:* Pathmakers use their independent, original thinking to forge a path in a new direction. If this is your soul purpose, you probably have the gifts of originality and innovation, but sometimes you may feel lonely, misunderstood, and unsupported. Your job, however, is to believe in yourself and forge ahead. If this is your soul purpose, you are here to clear a new avenue in the dark, dense forest of the unknown, and to be a leader even when you have no followers. Pathmakers are usually old souls who have gained the ability to seek brand-new ways of tackling problems, which requires a fearless attitude married to a compassionate heart. If you are a pathmaker, be patient with yourself and others, and trust that, in time, those who are meant to will find the path you've created.

• *Messenger:* Messengers are here to deliver important ideas to the world. This may happen in many ways. They may help a group of family, friends, or coworkers learn to see the world in a new and spiritual way. They may bring a message to a certain group or individual, or they may write something that helps a larger audience grow and embrace their path. Messengers tend to be connected to their spirituality at an early age. They are usually the vocal ones in the family because of their ability to see a problem, call it out, and then work to heal it. They often have a no-nonsense approach to life because of their gift for cutting through illusions to get to the heart of a problem. They see the big picture in all situations and help others do the same. If this is your soul purpose, people will learn from your life experiences and embrace your message of love, hope, and peace.

• *Builder:* Builders are here to create something from the ground up. This may be something literal—carpenters, architects, and designers often have this soul purpose. Or it may mean being an entrepreneur and building a business or enterprise. This purpose may manifest in different ways throughout different stages of life, and sometimes involves helping others build relationships or new ways of team-building and working together. Builders tend to be great bosses, leaders, and team players. If this is your soul purpose, you may come up with an idea that helps others discover a new way of seeing situations and themselves. However this gift manifests for you, rest assured that you have it within you to accomplish whatever you put your mind to.

- *Innovator:* Innovators are here to use their unique ideas and perspectives to effect change. They formulate new ideas and new ways of believing, as well as ideas and strategies that change the way others view themselves and the world around them. They encourage others to act in transforming and powerful ways. They are not meant to "fit in." Their innovating energy helps others realize and accept their own individuality, but sometimes they have to learn how to value their unique ideas and beliefs. If you are an innovator, your ideas will alter the way "normal" life operates around you. You may be an inventor or an entrepreneur. Working a traditional job may not always be the best option for you, although your innovating energy may initiate change in other ways—for instance, changing a policy at work or introducing a petition to amend a law. Simply by embracing your unique self, you can empower others to do the same. This soul purpose reminds me of one of my favorite quotes: "If you don't feel that you fit into this world, it's because you're here to create a new one."

- *Light-worker:* Light-workers agree to share their light with others to help them overcome fear and illusions of disconnection. If you are a light-worker, you are probably an old soul who has volunteered to come to Earth and use this lifetime to anchor down the light where you live. You may be naturally intuitive and empathic. You may be drawn to mystical studies, metaphysics, and spirituality. Lightworkers use their light in ways that are unique to them. But because they are natural givers and are here to serve the planet, they often forget to recharge their batteries and replenish their own light. Because they are connected to nature, however, they can easily recharge their energy and fill up their light just by spending time in the natural world.

- *Counselor:* Counselors are here to be listeners and guides for others. This doesn't mean they have to become literal counselors, however. It just means that they have the gift of validating others' experiences so that they feel heard and recognized. People with this soul purpose are rarely judgmental. They honor others' choices and journeys, and this helps others to trust them and consequently to trust themselves. Counseling also involves being present for others—witnessing their pain, validating their experiences, and listening to their fears and hopes without offering advice or opinions. It is in this silent listening that they do their best healing.

Recalling Your Soul Purpose

When we're born, the fontanel—the bones at the top of the skull—are not fully formed and there is space between them. There's a scientific reason for this, of course, but I've always liked to think of this space—the seat of the crown chakra—as our connection to source and a reminder that we should stay open to the divine. Children are born intuitive and spiritual, although they gradually lose these gifts as they acclimate to life in their physical bodies. But that connection to source is always with us. We just have to learn how to quiet the noise of life and go within to listen to our hearts. When we take time to reflect on who we were as children, before society told us who we should be, we start to reclaim our authentic selves and recall our soul purpose.

When I teach a Reiki class and show students the Reiki symbols, someone invariably says: "I remember doing this as a child." One student told me: "When I was a kid, my dog hurt his paw running over oyster shells on the beach. I remember holding him in my lap and putting my hands around his paw. I felt my hands heat up. Was I always a healer?" Another student, upon learning the spiraling shape of the *cho ku rei* symbol, said she used to doodle that exact symbol on her notebooks in school.

Children's behaviors are often an indicator of their soul purpose. One client who is now a minister grew up in an agnostic home. His favorite game as a child was "playing church." He set up an altar, laid a white T-shirt over it, and gave his siblings cookies and grape juice. "I don't even know where I learned to do that," he told me. "My parents never took us to church." But his soul knew that he was destined to serve as a minister.

A childhood friend of mine always volunteered to help others. She filled lunch bags with juice boxes, fruit, and soaps, and delivered them to homeless shelters. She volunteered for Special Olympics every year and taught herself to sew just so she could make blankets for animal shelters. Today, she's a successful fundraiser and grant-writer.

Sometimes it can take years to recall your soul purpose, and it often occurs in the face of tragedy. One client who had been a stay-at-home mom was shocked to learn that her husband had a completely separate and secret life. After going through a painful divorce, she started to run each morning before her children woke up, joking that she was simply trying to run away from her problems. But soon she realized that she loved running. She went on to get a degree in counseling and now runs a successful coaching business that trains people to heal through exercise and talk therapy.

Sometimes we discover new soul purposes as we move through the chapters of our lives. One podcast listener who worked as a veterinarian had always loved animals and was happy in her field. But in her free time, she devoured self-help books. Eventually, she was inspired to write her own and now works as a successful writer.

The key to recalling your soul purpose is to look at what makes your heart sing. You may find clues in your childhood, or in your hobbies and passions. Perhaps you're still learning about your soul purpose and haven't fully recalled it yet. That's okay too. Maybe you've fulfilled one soul purpose and are now moving on to another. This is the exciting aspect of seeing life as a school. You can always change your major and begin a new course of studies.

Expressing Your Soul Purpose

The way you choose to express your soul purpose is up to you. When a client learned one of her soul purposes was as a motivator, she protested at first, saying: "But

I'm just a realtor." When she thought about her life in terms of this soul purpose, however, she realized that she'd been motivating people her whole life. In high school, she had been class president. In college, she had run cross-country and helped her teammates achieve great success in their competitions. Her first job was in pharmaceutical sales, where she won many awards as best salesperson thanks to her motivational skills. As a realtor, she was constantly motivating homeowners to list their homes with her. But more important, she was selected by the company's owner to travel to other branches and motivate fellow realtors during the recent economic downturn. While she would never have called herself a motivational speaker, she now realizes that she's been doing exactly that her whole life.

Your soul purpose may have nothing to do with your chosen career. Nonetheless, you are always expressing yourself through it. If you're here to innovate, then no matter what career you choose, you will always utilize your unique ideas to initiate necessary change. If you're here to create, even if you work as a dental hygienist by day, you will find ways to express yourself creatively through pottery, painting, baking, or writing. Even if you feel as if your journey has led you far away from your soul purpose, know that it is a part of you and you will always find a way to express your true gifts and talents—once you learn to listen to the desires of your heart, the stirring in your soul.

Light Lessons: Owning Your Passions

This exercise helps you identify your passions and make them a part of your life. Each day for a week, take pictures of at least two objects, activities, people, or images that make you feel happy, uplifted, hopeful, or inspired. At the end of the week, take a meditative moment to review your pictures and answer the following questions:

- What do these pictures have in common?
- What do these pictures say about me?
- Which picture is special to me and why?
- How do these pictures make me feel?

Then ask yourself whether this exercise was hard or easy for you. How did it make you feel each day to notice things, images, and people that make you happy?

CHAPTER 6

Clearing Challenges and Obstacles

Dear Soul,

Now that you've chosen your team of allies, selected your family members, and settled on your soul purpose, it's time to choose your life lessons, challenges, and potential blocks so you can achieve your purpose during your time on Earth. Please keep in mind that your mission is to graduate from our university as a stronger, more loving consciousness who's growing ever closer to the light from which you originated.

During your studies at the University of Earth, it's imperative to keep in mind that your aim is not necessarily to ace every test or rush through every course. Rather, you're here to learn your unique way of responding to stress and difficulties, and then to reflect on whether these strategies are working for you. If not, you must learn how to release your old patterns and seek new avenues for healing and evolving your soul. It is up to you to identify these challenges, face them with resiliency and compassion, and learn how to ask for help when needed.

Remember that you are never alone, dear soul, even when it feels as if you are. The majority of the challenges you will face at the University of Earth have been chosen by you before you enrolled here and are designed to help you achieve your personal goals and dreams.

BEING A STUDENT IN THIS SCHOOL CALLED EARTH IS not easy. That's just a simple fact. As Longfellow so beautifully reminds us: "Into each life some rain must fall." The first step in dealing with the difficult times and challenging situations you will inevitably encounter is to recognize that they are a part of life. If you choose to agonize over them—"Why me?" "This isn't fair"—you get stuck in an endless cycle of pity, blame, regret, anger, and sadness. The second step is just to sit for a moment with the pain. There is nothing more stubborn than pain. It demands to be felt, explored, and understood before it passes. Pushing down painful emotions, ignoring them, or spiritually bypassing them is never the solution. You must feel *all* of your feelings. When you hide from painful emotions, they may lurk in the dark, but they never go away.

Carl Jung called these repressed feelings the "shadow" and said that, if you don't confront and heal the shadow, it will direct your life. That's a big statement, so let's take a closer look at what Jung meant.

Unmasking the Shadow

Stop and think about all the choices you have made in your life that were ruled by fear instead of love or peace or acceptance. Did you turn down a job or career opportunity because you were afraid of the responsibility or the changes it might bring? Did you feel as if you didn't deserve accolades you received? Did you end a relationship too quickly because you were afraid of getting hurt? Have you let your fears talk you out of pursuing a dream before you even tried?

What would happen if you took time to unpack all your fears, hurts, regrets, and anger, and gave them the time and attention they deserve? What would your life look like if you traced each of your fears back to its origins? When were they created? Were they even created by you, or are you carrying them for your parents or grandparents?

Now let's consider the word "shadow" as a metaphor. What do shadows do for us? They give depth and dimension to the light. They help to make clear where the light shines. Shadows give depth to help create the illusion that paintings are real. Think about that for a moment. Shadows create the illusion of three dimensions on a two-dimensional surface. This means that all the fearful stuff your shadow self is telling you is an illusion presenting itself as a very real thing.

Your shadow is created when you're more focused on the persona you present to the world than you are on the whole person you truly are inside and out. In your attempt to hide from your shadow, you create a mask formed from societal expectations, cultural beliefs, and your own natural inclinations to please others and achieve some semblance of a successful life. This mask ultimately feels more real to you than your authentic self. You feed it every day with a steady diet of consumerism, personal fears, and the illusions of how you feel your life should look.

But the mask is not who you are. It's who you feel you should be. Take off that mask and get to know the real you. The true, authentic you—with all your talents, foibles, fears, hopes, worries, and dreams—will never lead you astray.

Befriending the Shadow

Now let's ask a different question. What would your life look like if you *befriended* your shadow?

The first step in befriending your shadow is simply to acknowledge that it's there. Look at your triggers, the things that make you angry or sad, the words people say or the thoughts you think that make you feel like hiding from the world or raging at it. Examine these shadowy emotions without judgment. Simply allow yourself to observe them and recognize them. For example, I call one of my shadow aspects "Know-it-all Sam." I feel as if I just have to *know* things. I'm not exactly a know-it-all, but when I'm completely uneducated on a topic, it really bugs me.

Once I recognized this aspect of myself, I just sat with it and asked myself where it came from. When was Know-it-all Sam born? Then I started remembering little snippets from my childhood. For example, when I was a child, my dad and I were watching *The Great Escape*—a movie based on a true story about American POWs who tried to escape from a German prison camp in Poland by digging tunnels. I was horrified at what these men endured and said something like: "Those Germans were awful." My dad responded by telling me that we had done something similar to Japanese-Americans by putting them in internment camps. I had never heard of this and watched with shame as my dad got all puffed up and said: "You didn't know that? How could you not know that?" I felt like saying: "Because I am nine years old, Dad." But I didn't. I just swallowed the shameful feeling of not knowing something I *should* have known.

Once at a family dinner, my father was going on about how amazing it was that England—this tiny, rainy island—was able to be such a strong world leader for so long. When a family member admitted not knowing that England is an island, everyone else at the table thought that was hilarious. How could you not know England is an island? I still feel ashamed when I think about how I laughed along with my father.

Sometimes your shadow is born, not out of criticism you received as a child, but out of praise. As I was growing up, the only time I ever received positive attention from my mom was when I looked pretty. So today, one aspect of my shadow is a vain, annoying, preening little ball of darkness who rarely if ever leaves the house without makeup and who always tries to look her best. If you were the athlete in your family and were constantly praised for your prowess on the field, you may have a competitive shadow lurking in your subconscious. If you were the loyal do-gooder in your family, you may have a shadow that tells you to play small and focus on others' needs first.

You can start to acknowledge your shadow by looking at where you were praised in your life as a child, where you were criticized, and who did most of this praising or criticizing. If it's one of your parents, think about this little nugget of truth: We tend to partner with those most like the parent with whom we had the biggest issue. If you had a dismissive, cold, or abandoning parent and you haven't befriended this aspect of your shadow, you may be attracting romantic partners who are also dismissive, cold, or abandoning. If you had a parent who only loved you when you looked beautiful or achieved academic or athletic success, you may keep choosing partners who will also love you only under these conditions—until you befriend that shadow aspect.

Once you've identified your main shadow aspects and taken the time to really think about where and when they were created, you can start to shift your focus. Ask your shadow how it is protecting you. Then consider whether the answer you receive is true. Remember—shadows are all about illusions, so the answer your shadow gives will most likely not be true at all. Nonetheless, it may reveal a lot.

For example, I had a client who could not deal with any type of confrontation. When facing any kind of conflict, her voice tightened, her hands shook, and she often started to cry. I asked her to think about where in her younger life she had felt silenced. She shared that her father was a rage-aholic and her mother was always trying to keep the peace. And this meant that she was told to be quiet all the time. The one time she did speak up for herself and her mother, her dad went tearing out of the house in a rage and got into a very bad car accident. The car was totaled, but he was fine. Still, her shadow kept telling her that when she speaks up for herself, bad things happen. I also find it interesting to note that she collected toy mice. What's smaller or meeker than a little mouse?

Once she recognized where her fear of confrontation originated and that her inability to deal with conflict was really her shadow's way of protecting her from something bad happening, she was able to befriend this meek side of herself and work with it. Eventually, she started confronting a friend who was a bit of an energy vampire. And then she scheduled a meeting with her boss to talk about getting paid for her overtime hours. Slowly but surely, she learned to see that confronting others, setting boundaries, and speaking her truth protected her a whole lot better than keeping silent ever had.

Some of our shadow aspects aren't so easy to hide. I'm a semi-reformed road-rager and, while this isn't technically a shadow side because other drivers definitely see this part of me when I beep my horn or glare at them as I pass them in the left lane, it is still an aspect of myself that I'm not proud of. I started to befriend this inner road-rager by first accepting that this was a part of me. Then I asked myself what I was really angry about when I got stuck behind a slow driver. And it finally hit me. I felt powerless. When I'm on a two-lane road stuck behind someone going eighteen miles an hour in a thirty-five-mile-an-hour zone, there's not a darn thing I can do about it. I am not in control of the situation, and I have no choice but to surrender to this slower driver. Once I recognized what lay at the core of my road rage, it just slipped away. I just started leaving at least ten minutes earlier than I normally would so I wouldn't feel angry *and* impatient.

From Shadow into Light

Your shadow is really trying to be your friend. It is trying to protect you from feeling powerless, out of control, trapped, criticized, shamed, or belittled. The only problem is that, in trying to protect you from these negative emotions, it actually traps you in an illusion—the false persona or mask you present to the world. The more you ignore these shadow aspects of yourself, the more their negative suggestions appear to be true. You have to let them out into the light and see in them the gifts of truth and healing they're trying to offer you. You need to tell them that you see them, even as they try to hide in the dark recesses of your soul. You know why you created them and understand that they're trying to protect you. But you need to invite them to come out into the light so you can figure out this thing called life together.

You need to become an enlightened witness to the fears within you. Ask yourself what scared you as a child. Where did you feel powerless? What did you not allow yourself to feel? Where do you feel powerless now? Remember the old adage: "The truth shall set you free."

Remember this as you try to move through the pain of difficult life chapters.

In order to free yourself from the siren call of fear's illusions, you must look at yourself with naked honesty. At first, you may not like what you see—and that's okay. I wasn't exactly proud of Know-it-all Sam or my vanity or my inner road-rager. But once I embraced these two shadow aspects, I started to see how they had served me for a time. I wouldn't have achieved my academic success without the felt need to know everything. I wouldn't have focused on fitness and health if I weren't so vain. And if I weren't so darned impatient, it's possible I wouldn't have accomplished what I have so far in my life. When you can look at your naked self without judgment and see how your shadow aspects may have helped you in your life, you can start to incorporate them into your whole being.

Recently, I was complaining to a friend about a mutual acquaintance who's always bragging—calling, texting, or posting about her children's successes, her sales awards at work, her fabulous vacations, and on and on. My friend said: "You know Samantha, everything that annoys us about the people in our lives is a reflection of our personality we're trying to hide from." I felt the truth in that statement, but couldn't figure out how it applied to this situation. I am not a braggart. It's actually a point of honor for me *not* to brag. But I sat with what my friend had told me and thought about why this bragging acquaintance bugged me so much. She was not a reflection of my shadow side at all. Nowhere in the recesses of my mind is there a part of me yearning to shout from the rooftops about my children's good grades or the lovely trip to the mountains I just enjoyed.

But that weekend, I gave a presentation at a conference. There were lines of readers and listeners waiting to tell me how I'd positively impacted their lives. It was very overwhelming. Frankly, I had a hard time processing the beauty of the moment. I called my friend when I got back to the hotel and tried to explain how strange it felt to receive all this praise. Then I paused and said: "Anyway, tell me about your day." My friend said, "No. No more 'anyway.' Sit with this Samantha and take it in." That's when it hit me. I wasn't annoyed at my acquaintance for bragging. I was annoyed at *myself* for feeling as if I had no right in this world to brag. "Welcome," I said aloud to myself in the hotel room. "Welcome new shadow friend. It's nice to finally meet you in the bare light of truth."

Try it for yourself. Think about all the annoying things your friends, coworkers, and loved ones do that just really tick you off. Then sit with your annoyance and ask: "How is this a reflection of me?" The answer may not appear right away. But here's a fun fact I learned years ago. The subconscious mind can't handle unanswerable questions. Remember how, in the days before Google, when you tried to recall the title of a book or movie but couldn't no matter how hard you tried, the title would suddenly pop into your head hours, or even days, later? This is your subconscious mind at work. The one thing that drives it crazy is a question it can't easily answer. So when you take the time to sit with a question—Why does this person annoy me so much?—your mind will eventually yield answers. And perhaps you'll even get to meet a new shadow friend on your journey to self-love and true enlightenment.

Reframing Challenges

Most of the challenges you encounter in life were outlined by you and your team of allies before you came to Earth. They were designed by you to enable your soul to grow stronger. And since you enjoy free will, you can change aspects of your soul plan while in this school called life. But this also means that unexpected people and events can interject themselves into your life even though they weren't a part of your plan. Sometimes bad things just happen, and part of being a good student at the University of Earth is learning to accept all of this.

The crucial part of learning to handle life's challenges isn't understanding *why* these things happen. It's understanding *how* they happen. It's not important to understand why something is happening to you; what's more important is how you respond to what's happening to you. When you think about it, everything in your life comes down to your responses, your perceptions, and, finally, your actions. Not your *reactions*. Your actions. When you move from reacting to what life hands you (or throws at you) into an energy of grace where you pause and reflect and then take action, you are learning how to handle the best and worst that life has to offer.

Difficult times tend to help us grow more than happy times. When I was teaching poetry, my students always lamented that the poems we studied were all so sad and melancholy. I answered that, when you're sad, you take time to think and write and reflect. When you're happy, on the other hand, you're just in the moment being happy and joyful. We never stop to write about how great we feel. It's during the sad, scary, lonely times that we're forced to take a break from the hamster wheel of life and go within.

And this is where all the magic happens. Nature is constantly trying to teach us this. A butterfly grows through the hungry, cramped, scary changes that happen in the dark cocoon. A diamond emerges from charcoal that's been placed under extreme stress. An annoying piece of sand trapped in an oyster shell transforms into a prized pearl. After a dark and dreary storm, a beautiful rainbow appears.

Painful times are just one way that your soul cries out to you. When you stub your toe, your body sends a painful message to your brain so you learn to be more careful when you're rushing out the door. In the same way, emotional pain serves as a reminder to be gentler with yourself as you move through the world. Pain strengthens you, pushes you, prods you to keep going, or encourages you to take a needed break. C. S. Lewis called pain "God's megaphone," something used only in dire times to get your attention. When you're facing a difficult chapter in your life, take a moment to ask what these events are trying to tell you. Are you being encouraged to make a big change? To take a leap of faith? To walk away or move toward something new?

As my marriage came to an end, I was loathe to face the truth of this. I didn't want to raise my children in a "broken" family; yet things kept happening in my life that made me see that this was the only choice I had. I believe that my breast cancer diagnosis, which occurred in the middle of my marriage crisis, helped me to grow in strength and independence so that I could make the final, painful decision to end the marriage. I didn't see that as I was going through the experience, however. I had to rely on my faith to get me through, knowing that everything was happening to me and for me in order for growth and inner healing to occur.

That's the tricky thing about these dark nights of the soul. We often can't see the light that they're trying to shine on us until we've gotten through the darkness on our own. We just have to hold on to a grain of faith, a mustard seed of hope, knowing and trusting that all of this pain, loss, fear, and suffering are molding us into a lighter, truer version of who we are.

It's also important to recognize challenging aspects of your life that keep repeating themselves, as these may be life challenges that your soul chose before you were born. Until you recognize them for what they are, they will keep repeating, perhaps showing up in different guises. But sometimes just recognizing them is the first step toward healing them.

Years ago I was complaining to a friend about a difficult boss. While I loved my job, my boss did not love me. She admonished me if I was even a little late; but if I arrived early, she accused me of trying to "steal overtime money." She was consistently rude and belittling, making my work life a veritable hell. When I told my friend that this was the third mean boss I'd had in row, she said: "You know Samantha, there's a pattern here." I laughed a little and admitted that I did seem to attract mean bosses. "No, that's not it," she replied. "All these bosses have been angry, older women. This is the Universe's way of telling you to deal with your angry mom."

That was a huge *aha* moment for me. I realized that all my bosses were exactly like my mother. Soon after, I found a good therapist and learned how to set (and keep) boundaries with my mom. After that, the challenges I was experiencing in my work world seemed to disappear as if by magic. The minute I recognized the repeating pattern and worked hard to reframe it, my life changed for the better.

Responding vs. Reacting

During these dark nights of the soul, it's imperative to practice the power of the pause. The world we live in is often noisy and chaotic, sometimes rude, and filled with demands and expectations. We're told to be tuned in and plugged in all the time—to work, friends, social media, current events. This can leave us feeling disconnected, alone, misunderstood, and overwhelmed. But the world we live in is never going to just slow down and stop. We are the ones who have to slow down and stop. During challenging times, we have to give ourselves permission to pause long enough to formulate a response, rather than just immediately reacting.

There's a big difference between responding and reacting. Reacting is about feeling defensive. Responding is about being conscious and connected to the moment. When you pause to take a breath and focus on how you want to respond to a situation rather than just reacting to it, you stay in control of the situation. When you react, you lose your cool, you resort to old instincts and act out of preconceived notions. You stop listening. You lose your filter.

When you react, you don't think. You allow your unconscious to take over, which can lead to hurtful words or actions. When you respond, you take a moment to explore options, to look at both sides. You give yourself a chance to breathe. You allow yourself to listen and be heard. When you respond rather than just reacting, you have a chance to ask some important questions. Is this really about me? What's actually happening here? Am I seeing this challenge clearly? Is this person trying to start a fight to distract me from something bigger? Am I trying to create an issue to avoid focusing on something I need to address? Is this really even a challenge, or am I allowing myself to be triggered? Answering these questions gives you time to take a step back and engage the situation rationally and calmly.

Be Kind to Yourself

Another crucial aspect of dealing with life's challenges is learning to be kind to yourself through the tough times. Too often, we blame ourselves for the bad things that happen to us. If you get into a car accident, you blame yourself for not paying attention. If you fall into debt, you blame yourself for spending too much or not earning enough. When a relationship ends, you blame yourself for not doing enough.

After my divorce, it was very hard for me to learn how to be a single mother. I went to bed every night feeling as if I would never catch up with all the things on my to-do lists. One sleepless night, I sat up in bed and wrote down a timeline of the events I'd been through in the last ten years. I felt that I needed to see them on paper as a way of telling myself to calm down. I'd been through a lot and I knew I was doing my best. But somehow, that didn't seem to be enough.

When I finished my timeline, I was shocked to see how much change had been thrust upon me in a short time—my ex-husband's shooting and recovery, my breast cancer, a devastating hurricane, my parents illness and need for weekly assistance from me. As I sat in my bed that night staring at my timeline, I started to feel the cold, hard shell of self-blame and recrimination melt away from me.

Try it for yourself. Identify all the significant events, both positive and "negative," that have occurred through-out your life. Write down the positive events in one color and the challenging events in another. Are there more positive events or more challenging events? Can you see any repeating patterns? Evaluate the challenges you've experienced and look for patterns there. If the same kind of negative situations or people keep popping up for you, try to get to the root source of these challenges. Do they remind you of a situation from your childhood? Are they highlighting a shadow aspect of yourself that needs to be unmasked? Do they represent a negative lesson you learned from your family of origin?

Once you see the source of your repeating challenges, look honestly within yourself and try to determine positive, healthy action steps you can take right now to change this pattern. It can also help to identify patterns in your life that may be recurring to teach you a lesson of surrender, letting go, or acceptance.

Healing Your Inner Child

Most of our challenges are rooted in childhood. Whether it's a traumatic event, or a difficult move, or a negative homelife fraught with yelling or cold silences, or bullies at school, we all have something in our childhood that needs to be healed. Working backward through these events and situations to heal your inner child can reap beautiful rewards in your current life.

When you hold on to pain from childhood, you continue to re-experience that pain in adulthood until you can learn to heal your inner child. Studies show, for example, that, if your father leaves your family and abandons you, you have a higher chance of either marrying someone who will abandon you or becoming the one who abandons your loved ones. When my father was in rehab recovering from alcohol addiction, a counselor told me: "Unless you release your pain now, you will either grow up to become an alcoholic or marry one." I am very happy to report that I did release the pain and continue to do so whenever something from my childhood pops up. And I did not become an alcoholic, nor did I marry one. Having the knowledge that these patterns could be repeated kept me vigilant and focused on making positive choices.

The things that happen to us as children remain magnified within us because, as children, we are essentially powerless. We are at the mercy of our parents. If they have a bad day, guess who else is going to have a bad day? Moreover, children don't have the capacity to see things beyond themselves, so they perceive everything as their fault. If dad leaves, a five-year-old believes he did something wrong. If mom gets drunk every afternoon, a nine-year-old believes it's her fault. Many adults who are raised in dysfunctional homes become either over-achievers or under-achievers, some always trying hard to fix problems and others feeling as if there's no point in doing so.

I had a client who continually dated men who messed up her life. The problem was that they all did this in different ways, so it took her a frustratingly long time to see the pattern. Her father had never left the home, but he checked out emotionally after declaring bankruptcy and seeing his long-held dream of owning his own business go down the drain. My client was only six when he stopped being a participant in her life. All her memories revolve around him coming home from work, eating in silence, and watching TV until he fell asleep in a recliner.

Her mother eventually acted out by having affairs. When she grew up, she began dating men who couldn't connect with her emotionally (just like her dad), and who always created drama (just like her mom). One boyfriend was a gambler, another was a serial cheater; one lied about everything (including his marriage and two children); one began stalking her after she broke up with him. We always re-create the sadness from our childhood until we face it and heal the inner child who is still in there waiting to be loved. We repeat the pattern until we learn to forgive ourselves.

CRYSTALS FOR HEALING THE INNER CHILD

- Smithsonite helps release painful childhood memories.
- Yellow chalcedony works to strengthen inner confidence while helping you reclaim childlike joy.
- Rhodonite is a powerful heart healer that helps release grief and heartache.
- Blue calcite brings more peace and clarity by prompting clear communication and helping calm emotions.
- Pink danburite opens, clears, and awakens the heart chakra to focus on love and self-love.

So how can you do that? First you have to escape from the land of denial. I see so many clients who claim to have experienced a perfect childhood and can't see what that has to do with all the chaos in their present lives. But while they may have had great childhoods and been raised by wonderful, hands-on parents, there is always some pain that needs to be released. One of my friends had amazing parents. I often envied the love and adoration they bestowed on her. But when she changed schools, she was picked on horribly for being the "new kid." She was bullied and even had her arm broken on the school bus. Obviously, this had a terrible effect that continued to haunt her as an adult. Her self-esteem was crushed. She eventually learned to heal from this through therapy, writing, and acting.

Look at the patterns in your life. Where are your worries constantly focused? Health? Money? Relationships? Career? If you have a lot of health issues, it may mean you weren't properly nurtured and cared for as a child. Money issues center on feelings of self-worth. Who told you that you weren't worth much? If you have relationship issues, examine your parents' relationship to each other and to their peers. If you have career problems, ask yourself if anyone ever told you that you were special, that you could do anything, be anything you wanted to be. Once you've identified your pattern, work to heal it through guided imagery, therapy, writing, and affirmations.

There are many things you can do to heal your inner child. Try writing a letter to your inner child explaining how much you are loved and protected and safe. Write back using your nondominant hand. Indulge in child-like behaviors—play, color, imagine, skip, daydream, sleep with a teddy bear or body pillow. Ask your parents about their childhoods so you can begin to understand them as people rather than just as your parents. Spend some time imagining the childhood you wish you'd had. For example, if you could grow up in any sitcom family, which one would you choose? *Modern Family? The Middle? Family Ties? Growing Pains? Happy Days? The Brady Bunch?*

Imagine the home you wish you'd had and put yourself there as a small child. Visualize the parents you wish you'd had, telling you how loved and special you are. Create a healing collage. Glue on pictures of yourself as a child and surround them with affirmations of love and healing. Hang it up somewhere private where you can see it every day—your closet or bedroom. In the morning and evening, stare at your collage and send love to your inner child.

Surrendering the Need to Be Right

In my work, I've witnessed so much needless fighting and suffering over the need to be right. A few months ago, I was connecting a client to her mom, who'd passed away almost twenty years before. The mom was sad because my client hadn't spoken to her sister in years, and showed me a diamond ring that was broken in half to symbolize the conflict with the sister. When I relayed this to my client, she scoffed: "It's more than one diamond ring. My sister took my mom's engagement ring and diamond wedding bands when she died, even though she wanted us to divide everything equally." When I asked the woman what it would take for her to talk to her sister again—because it seemed that was the only thing the mother wanted—she replied: "She'd have to tell me she was wrong for taking the rings." Was it really worth losing a relationship over something like this? That's not for me to say. But it is a good question to ponder if you've fallen out with people in your life.

Sometimes people get so stuck on their need to be right that they lose sight of what's important. I had a client who was clearly wronged by her ex-husband. Not only did he cheat on her, but he would never admit it and certainly would never apologize for breaking his marital vows. As she watched him get remarried and start a new family, she wallowed in a stew of bitterness and anger. These negative emotions started to affect her work, her friendships, and her mental health. I told her that he would likely never apologize and gently suggested that it was time to accept this and move on with the next chapter of her life. She refused, however, and even stated that she would never date again so he'd have to pay her alimony for the rest of his life. She maintained that the only way to inflict pain on her ex-husband was to "make him pay."

I encouraged her to change this way of thinking because, if she didn't, nothing else would change in her life. She would remain stagnant, stuck, and bitter. She could stay stubbornly focused on her quiet revenge plan, but that wouldn't let her move on in her own life. I told her that I saw love waiting around the corner, but it would stay waiting until she could surrender this need to be right and have her revenge—however just.

She returned to me a year later, ready to work on letting some of this go. Together we wrote down a list of all the pain and hurt her ex-husband had caused her. Then we burned the paper and buried the ashes. This allowed her to see the ending of this relationship as a symbolic death that needed to be grieved, healed, and released. I also encouraged her to repeat the affirmation "I let you go with love and peace in my heart" whenever she had to think about or deal with her ex-husband, and suggested that she wear rose quartz as a reminder that she was open to love and healing.

I'm happy to report that she returned to my office a year later with a smiling, handsome man by her side and a beautiful engagement ring on her finger. What would her life have looked like if she hadn't made the decision to release this need to be right and vindicated? How would your life be different if you took steps to surrender the need to be right?

Holding on to past pains is often like having a sore that you can't help touching. It hurts, and the more you touch it, the worse the pain gets. But you can't help yourself. If you want to heal from the challenges life has tossed into your path, you have be willing to release the pain, to release the need to be right, to surrender the apology you may never receive.

I speak here from personal experience. When I was going through my divorce, I am sure I sounded like a broken record to my friends and family. I constantly listed all the reasons I'd been wronged and how unfair it all felt. I sounded like a tired, cranky three-year-old. My favorite lament was: "But it's not fair!" And then a friend said to me: "Samantha, you need a tiny violin, some balloons, and a chocolate cake so you can throw yourself a pity party to go along with your whining." It wasn't exactly the comfort and validation I was seeking, but she was right. Her words struck me like Cher slapping Nicholas Cage in that scene from *Moonstruck* and telling him: "Snap out of it!" And so I did.

Instead of ruminating on the past and bemoaning the present, I thought about the future. I imagined my children's college graduations, their weddings, their future families. I didn't want to celebrate those milestones without their father. So I called him up and said: "I want to stop fighting. I don't care who's right and who's wrong. I just know that I want you by my side when we walk our daughters down the aisle and when we welcome our grandchildren into the world. We have to find a way to be friends." My pagan friends say that words are spells we cast into the world. Maybe so, because those words magically changed our relationship. All the anger just went to the side, like water finding an open drain after a storm. My willingness to surrender the need to be right created a new path for a different kind of relationship for us.

Accept the challenges you're going through. Acknowledge the pain. And stop waiting for validation or an apology. When you take the time to recognize, embrace, and surrender to your challenges, you extend an open invitation to all the beauty, grace, and joy the Universe is waiting to give you.

Forgiveness

Forgiving is *for giving* yourself peace. You do not need to tell others you are forgiving them. They don't need to ask for forgiveness in order for you to grant it—although, admittedly, sometimes that would be nice. Forgiveness is about you, your lessons, your journey, your sense of self, your strength and peace. It is not about those who have hurt you.

Nor does forgiving mean forgetting, or else you risk the situation occurring again. When you forgive, you remember the event, but you do so without remembering the pain. Moreover, forgiveness is an ongoing process. It is a recurring emotion with which you may battle, but through the power of surrender, you ultimately walk across the bridge of freedom to the land of peace.

I'm not sure everything is forgivable. But I do feel it's important to try to forgive. Just the act of trying to let go of a painful memory can yield beautiful results. If you don't try to forgive, you are in jeopardy of continually being hurt, of experiencing the physical and emotional complications of anger and guilt, of staying stuck in a place of negativity, anger, and bitterness. You run the risk of getting caught in vengeful thoughts, of getting stuck in imaginary future defensive arguments, of being trapped by fear that the situation will occur again. Not forgiving those who have hurt you can even lead to physical symptoms like high blood pressure, chronic stress, headaches, immune disorders, anxiety, and low self-esteem. When you choose to forgive, you develop compassion, deepen your spirituality, and experience mental, emotional, and physical health.

Here are some simple steps for discovering the power of forgiveness in a painful situation. They are based on the acronym GRACE:

- **Gratitude:** Meditate on the blessings in the situation, how you've grown and the lessons you've learned. Focus on how this has empowered you and helped you discover yourself.

- **Respect:** Respect the enormity of the situation and give yourself time to process your emotions. Don't just move on. And don't diminish the experience. You've got to give yourself time to feel your feelings. Validate your negative emotions before you transform them into positive ones.
- **Accept:** Accept the reality of the situation. Don't fight it, ignore it, complain about it, or defend it. Simply accept what has happened to you so the healing can begin.
- **Create:** Create new opportunities for yourself. Get out, reach out, give, and serve.
- **Enlist help:** Ask for help from friends, family, and your prayer life.

Light Lessons: Meditation to Surrender and Forgive
This meditation is designed to help you surrender any blocks forged in your heart from a lack of forgiveness. Read it into a voice-recording app and fall asleep to the sound of your voice encouraging your subconscious mind to forgive, release, and let go.

You are walking through a beautiful garden when you come across four cages, each containing a white dove. On each cage is the name of someone you need to forgive. Walk up to the first cage and unlock it. As you watch the dove fly free, say: "I forgive you. I forgive you and I set you free." Go to the next cage and read the name printed there. Open the cage and watch the dove soar high into the sky as you say: "I forgive you. I forgive you and I set you free." On the next cage, you see the name of an event you need to release. Unlock that door and say: "I surrender the pain connected to this event. I retain the lessons, but I set the rest free."

On the last cage, you're surprised to see your own name. Open that cage and watch that dove of peace and joy happily fly free as you say: "I forgive myself. I forgive myself and I set myself free."

Feeling light and renewed, you continue on your walk and come across a beautiful waterfall. Walk under this waterfall and know that, as the water cleanses you, it is releasing any and all residue of people or events you need to forgive. Feel the healing energy of the waters cleanse your mind, your body, and your soul.

When you are ready, continue walking until you come to a clearing in which you see a beautiful temple surrounded by columns. This is a healing temple. If you need help going into the temple, ask your angel to come and be by your side. When you're ready, begin walking up the stairs leading to the top of this beautiful temple. When you get to the top, you see many people from your life whom you've forgiven and who have forgiven you, and many whom you still need to forgive. Spend some time here embracing everyone and feeling the love and joy that comes from this healing place of peace.

When you are ready, walk inside the temple. The walls are a beautiful emerald green and the color seems to vibrate with healing energy. With each breath, you feel more peaceful. You walk into a large room and realize it's a theater. On the stage in front of you is the person you most need to forgive. Don't be afraid of this confrontation. Breathe easily. Walk down the aisle toward the stage. See this person slowly shrink and become a five-year-old child again. Take some time here to get out all your emotions. Tell this person all the effects his or her behavior has had on you. Release your anger, your sadness, your regret, everything.

When you have exhausted yourself, take a minute to listen to what this person's inner child has to say to you. Listen with an open heart.

You both notice a golden box lying on the stage. You discuss with each other all the "should haves" and "could haves" and "would haves" and "maybes" connected with the situation that needs forgiveness and put them all in this golden box. Place all your lost dreams and broken hopes in the box as well. And listen as the child puts his or her lost dreams and shattered hopes into the box too.

When you are ready, you both walk off the stage and go out a back door to a beautiful forgiveness garden, taking the golden box with you. All around, you see lush roses, tulips, daffodils, and lilies. Smell the fragrant flowers, then kneel on the ground with this small child and dig a hole. Together, place the golden box in the hole and cover it with fresh soil. Stand up and hold the child's hand as you watch a bouquet of flowers magically grow from the soil. Turn to the child and say: "I forgive you." Then tell the child what you are forgiving.

Feel the love and sense of peace growing inside of you. Know that you've planted a seed inside yourself that, when you're ready, will bloom into a bouquet of serenity and inner happiness. Tell the child that you also forgive yourself, and then give a warm hug. As you continue hugging, see the child grow into an adult again. A warm, loving pink light descends around you both, wrapping you in its loving embrace. Feel all your anger and hurt and sadness melt away into this pink light. See the other person's anger and hurt and sadness also dissolve into the soft, loving pink light.

After a moment, walk out of the forgiveness garden, back into the theater, and out through the temple doors. Walk slowly down the stairs, feeling lighter and freer with each step. Walk past the cleansing waterfall, knowing you can come back here at any time to wash away any negative emotions. Stroll past the empty dove cages and feel the exquisite joy of knowing that you have released all unforgiven issues from your body, mind, and soul.

You feel a sense of peaceful empowerment, knowing that you can return to this place at any time to release negative emotions and experience the healing power of forgiveness.

When you're ready, begin to come back into your body and flutter your eyes open.

CHAPTER 7

Amending Your Soul Plan

Dear Soul,

Now that you've worked on the majority of your soul plan, it's important to remember that, once you get to the University of Earth, you can amend this plan to suit the needs of your growing, evolving self. Too many souls forget this and choose instead to stay stuck in areas of their lives that no longer serve them, necessitating a return to this difficult university for remedial courses.

This need not be the case for you, as long as you remember to call on your team for help. It is of primary importance that you stay ever cognizant of the fact that you are a powerful co-creator capable of enormous change, healing, and growth.

WHEN YOUR SOUL PLAN IS CREATED IN THE SAFETY and unconditionally loving environment of heaven, it all seems easy and doable. But once you arrive on Earth, all bets are off because your plan bumps up against the soul plans of everyone you encounter. Think of planning the perfect vacation. You book the flights and hotel, plan out the restaurants, reserve tickets for shows you want to see, pack all your clothes, and even remember your travel toothbrush. This is going to be the perfect vacation! Then your plane is delayed so you miss your connecting flight. The hotel loses your reservation. And it rains every day. This is how life can feel once you've arrived at the school of life. You've planned everything the way it's supposed to go—fate. But you just never know what will happen once you get here to Earth—free will.

The fate versus free will debate has been argued for millennia. Many religions teach that all of our life events are fated. One Sufi poem tells us: "God long ago drew a circle in the sand exactly around the spot where you are standing right now. You were never not coming here." This thought both terrified and comforted me when I first read it. It's frightening to think that we're not in control of anything in our lives—that fate's hand dictates the course of our lives as if we're nothing more than puppets on a stage. But it can also be comforting to realize that we're exactly where we're supposed to be, that life is organizing and working itself out in our favor.

For years, scientists adopted the determinist view that every event is predetermined by prior events working in conjunction with the laws of nature. But quantum physics is proving that this is simply not true. A phenomenon called the "observer effect" has shown that, when particles are observed in a laboratory setting, they act differently based on who's observing them. Authors like Lynne McTaggart have carried this scientific finding over into research about how our words, thoughts, and intentions can change the course of the world around us. Although fate suggests that everything is predetermined—already set in stone—she argues that this is completely opposite to the quantum universe in which we live, which shows us that we are co-creating as we go. In the quantum world, subatomic particles are merely *potential*. From this, she concludes that we all have unlimited potential and share a destiny for great things.

Fate and Free Will

In fact, we live in a world in which fate and free will *co-exist*. The key is to recognize which events in your life are fated and which are born from your will's free choices and actions. Think of the story of the man who dreamed one night that a terrible storm would come and wipe away his village. Believing in fate, he put his trust in God to protect him. Sure enough, the next day the flood waters arrived. On the first day of the storm, when his brother begged him to flee to safety, he replied that God would protect him. On the second day, when his neighbor offered to take him to safety along with his own family, he shook his head and claimed that God would protect him. By the third day, the waters had risen so high that the man was forced to take refuge on his roof. When a group of villagers came by in a boat and pleaded with him to come with them, he refused because he believed God would protect him.

The man was eventually washed away by the flood waters and drowned. When he got to heaven, he shouted at God in rage: "Why didn't you help me as you promised?" And God replied: "I sent your brother, your neighbor, and even a boat to save you, but you declined my help." The storm was fated to happen. But how the man responded to the storm was a matter of free will. He chose to ignore the offers of help. Think about the times in your own life when you may have done the same thing.

It can be hard to recognize the hand of fate in our own lives. We often can't see our destiny until fateful events have already occurred. In the months leading up to my ex-husband's shooting, we had many signs. I had recurring precognitive dreams of the event. I kept finding heart-shaped seashells on the beach. I knew it was a message that my family and I were surrounded by love and support, but I couldn't shake the ominous feeling that surrounded me when I gathered up those shells. On the night of the shooting, I begged him several times not to go to work, but he insisted on going because several officers in his platoon were either out sick or on vacation or away for training. So when he faced the shooter that night, he was all alone. Was that fate? Was this dreadful event that changed our family's lives destined to happen? And if so, was it also destined that he would live?

Many things transpired that night to make my husband live. An ambulance on another call right down the road from the shooting provided the life-saving care he needed almost instantly. The exact thoracic surgeon he needed was on call at the hospital when he arrived. When he needed a blood transfusion, the right blood type was there without having to send out for it. For months, I believed that, for whatever reason, it was fated that he would be shot that night, but that it was also fated that he would survive. This brought me enormous comfort as we faced the difficult months of recovery.

But then I was gifted a reading by a well-known medium who told me that I had called someone back from heaven. I didn't know what she was talking about and asked for clarification. She shrugged and replied: "I'm not really sure, but someone was supposed to die. I can see someone in a hospital bed surrounded by tubes and wires. He was supposed to die, but your prayers called him back."

I thought back to those first nights when my ex-husband was in a coma fighting for his life, and all his fellow officers crowded the corridors of the hospital. I called it the "sea of blue." These men and women were his family as much as I was. So, despite doctors' objections, I allowed them to visit him, with this caution: "Don't tell him not to die. Hold his hand and tell him to live." I knew the power of words and intentions and I wanted him to remember the promise he'd made to his family—that no matter what happened to him on the job, he'd fight to live.

When the medium told me that I'd called someone back from heaven, it made me question the fate versus free will issue all over again. Was it fated that he was shot and survived that night? Yes. Was it also the result of free will—choices freely made and actions freely taken—that he walked out of that hospital alive? Possibly. And there's the rub. That's the toughest part of being a human. We just don't know. We have to surrender so much while we are here on Earth in order to receive the beautiful blessings life has to offer. We may never know why he was shot that night, just as you may never understand why you got sick or divorced or fired. And then we get stuck in the *whys*. Why did this happen? Why couldn't I prevent this? Why didn't I do more? Why didn't God answer my prayer? Why didn't anyone intervene to help? Why, why, why.

But there's very little power in the *why*. The why is weak and uncertain, filled with doubt and insecurity. Leaning into your why will not help you move forward. It will keep you stuck in a cycle of blame, criticism, shame, and regret. All your power lies instead in the *how*. How will you respond to this fateful event? How will you grow as a result of what's transpired? How will you heal from this? How will you gather the help and support you need now? How will you make the changes you need to make in order to move on? How will you turn around and help others get through similar experiences?

There's an oft-told tale about a woman who visits a psychic to ask how she's going to die. When the psychic tells her she will die in a car crash, she vows never to leave her house again for fear of dying in a crash. She spends years hiding away in her house convinced that she's avoiding her fate. Then one night, a drunk driver crashes into her home and kills her as she lies sleeping in her bed.

The moral of this story is that you can't avoid your fate. Your power lies in your ability to make choices. This woman could have chosen to live her days outside enjoying life. But she didn't. She chose to cower alone inside her house, avoiding life—ironically, so she could live. Look around at people who are living lives that are so much smaller than they should be, simply because they fear their fate. How many do you know who stay in miserable marriages because they don't want to be alone or move or lose money? How many work at jobs they hate because they fear the unknown of the next job? It all comes down to resistance—resistance against what you perceive as your destiny. But remember: What you resist persists. Fear is the biggest obstacle you'll encounter in your life. You must work to overcome your internal fears so that you can live the rich, beautiful life your soul planned for you. When you do, you can be the hero of your own life journey.

Three Gates to Enlightenment

Zen Buddhists teach that there are three gates to enlightenment—suffering, joy, and compassion—and that these gates teach you all you need to know about learning to accept your fate.

At the first gate, suffering, you learn that hardship is a part of life. Each and every one of us has experienced and will continue to experience suffering. The more you resist this fact, the more you suffer. But it's through suffering that you often receive the greatest blessings, insights, and growth. If you'd had a perfect childhood, you might not be the strong, resilient person you are now. If you'd never known loss, you might not have learned to appreciate the people in your life as much as you do. If you'd never gone through heartbreak, you might not understand and appreciate the beautiful depths of true love.

One story tells of a man who finds a butterfly struggling to emerge from its cocoon. He sits down and watches for hours as the butterfly tries to break free.

Eventually, he can't watch the creature suffer anymore, so he takes a pair of scissors and carefully cuts the cocoon to free it. The butterfly emerges effortlessly from the cocoon and the man walks away feeling happy that he has helped it break free from suffering. But the butterfly's body is too small and its wings are so short and shriveled that it spends the rest of its life unable to fly.

Our instinct is to stop suffering when we encounter it. But the butterfly needed to suffer to pass through the tiny hole in the cocoon because that's nature's way of forcing fluid from the body of the butterfly into its wings so it can fly. Suffering works the same way for us. We often can't see the point of a difficult situation while it's happening, but it's always the Universe's way of making us better, stronger, and more resilient so we can soar to our next level of growth.

The second Zen gate is joy. This gate opens for you when you stop fighting your own suffering and that of the world. But the key is that you can't understand true joy until you've passed through the gate of suffering. Without knowing sadness and loss, you can't understand happiness and bliss. The gifts that come when you surrender to your fate may first appear as suffering. This is true and must be accepted. But eventually, your suffering morphs into the beautiful realization that life is miraculous, even in its darkest moments, because there's always a light waiting to lead you to the gate of joy.

Many try to ignore the first gate. They want to just skip right on by the gate of suffering and force their way through the gate of joy. And you can do this too. But when you bypass the suffering, you simply choose to live an illusion where real emotions, memories, and feelings are pushed down, down, down into the recesses of your heart. Like Dorothy waltzing down the yellow brick road to the mythical Land of Oz, this can only take you to a false sense of well-being. If you want to experience true joy, you must first settle into suffering and accept all the pain and beauty it's trying to give you, knowing and trusting that it's molding you into a stronger, better version of yourself. This is the only true path home to enlightenment.

Until you've experienced pain, loss, and recovery, and the joy of healing, you cannot pass through the third Zen gate—compassion. You can't empathize with other souls. When you ignore your suffering and try to focus only on joy, the result is a hollow, fleeting feeling. You move from moment to moment, vicariously holding on to the good times, but always wondering: "Why don't I feel truly happy? What is missing from my life?" Without the gift of suffering, you forget that we're all connected, that what happens to one of us, happens to all of us.

Suffering levels the playing field. It humbles and connects everyone and enables us to reach out a hand to others who are trying to pass through the gates of joy and compassion. When we've recovered from our own dark nights of the soul, we emerge feeling emboldened, more loving, and able to shine a beacon of light so that others can survive their dark times as well.

Compassion and Self-Love

One of my favorite cards in the tarot deck is the Hermit, which shows an old man standing atop a snowcapped mountain. The wintry season reflects how alone he has been, while the mountain behind him represents his achievements. He has gained wisdom during his solitary dark night of the soul. In one hand, he holds a staff representing the support and wisdom that comes from walking this Earth for many years. In his other hand, he holds a lantern signifying the light he's attained during his years of living alone. A six-pointed star lights up the lantern—the Star of Solomon—symbolizing the wisdom that can only be obtained by going within and choosing to pass through the gate of suffering.

The lantern only lights the Hermit's path for a few feet in front of him, however, reminding us that we can't know our futures. We can only be guided by the light within us—the light we've acquired through years of experiencing suffering, joy, and then compassion. This is the gift of learning to reach out to others for guidance and connection. This card reminds me that every bit of pain and joy I've experienced will be used to help others going through similar challenges, because the first two gates have taught me compassion and given me the tools I need to help others triumph over similar obstacles.

You can pass through the gate of compassion without first going through the gates of suffering and joy, but those who do never learn self-love. Instead, they focus on always helping others, sacrificing their own needs and healthy boundaries in an altruistic quest to be a savior to others. Part of learning to accept your fate involves learning to love yourself. And this includes loving the bad choices you make, the stupid decisions you thoughtlessly embrace, and the choices and opportunities you choose not to take out of fear. You can't be truly compassionate with others until you first learn to be loving and gentle with yourself.

Fighting vs. Acceptance

In our society, acceptance falsely masquerades as weakness. Many refuse to accept their fate because, to them, it feels like giving up. Yet, although there are times in your life when you have to fight for what and who you believe in, there are also times when you have to surrender and accept the destiny that fate is offering you. How do you know the difference? There's an ease and grace that comes when you're on the right path. Look for those moments in your life when events are flowing smoothly, even in the midst of conflict. This is your sign that you're doing the right thing.

When my husband was still in the hospital fighting for his life, the city manager contacted me to set up his worker's compensation benefit. When I said it was too soon to think about that, he replied: "Well, he's been here for twenty-one days. We only pay first-responders their full salary for twenty-one days, so he has to go on worker's comp." I was shocked. This man had sacrificed his health and his future for the city, and the city was already taking him off full salary. I had to take a leave of absence from my own job to raise our girls and focus on his recovery. We couldn't survive on his salary alone, never mind the incredibly low worker's compensation they were offering. But how could I battle city hall?

I wasn't ready to give up the fight just yet, however. I reached out to a student who had stopped by to visit me in the hospital and who had said causally as he left: "I'm kind of connected with local politics, so if you need help with anything, give me a call." I did. And I called a fellow officer's wife who'd also offered to help. Together the three of us went to every local group we could think of for assistance. Soon, without any resistance or planning, we had a large group supporting me as I went before the city council and asked for the twenty-one-day law to be amended. The amendment passed easily, and now all first-responders receive their full salary for one year following any major on-the-job injury. That was a good fight.

On the other hand, I've fought battles that were plagued by resistance, backlash, and obstacles. Here's a trivial example. One semester I had to deal with a class clown who constantly interrupted me to tell jokes or make fun of the subject we were discussing. He wasn't a bad student or a vindictive jokester. He was actually pretty funny. But his constant interruptions were impacting my class. I tried to fight him—allowing an awkward silence to fill the classroom each time he interjected his comments, or asking him to leave class, or even joking along with him hoping this would even out the energy in the room. None of it worked. Finally, I told him I would give him ten minutes at the beginning of each class to entertain us. In return, I demanded that he give me the rest of the class time to teach. He agreed. The class loved to start each day with laughter, and then we settled into learning literature.

Accepting fate entails learning to recognize the quiet, yet persistent, language of the Universe. I tell students in my classes on manifesting that, if it's meant to be, it will be easy. This has been true throughout my life. And if you look back on your own experiences, you'll see it's true for you as well. Life is about learning to know when it's time to fight and—just as important—when it's time to yield, accept, and surrender.

Unfortunately we have been taught to attach negative connotations to all these words. Yielding, acceptance, and surrender bring to mind images of losing, being weak, and giving up. But the strongest thing we can do is often to give up and walk away from a situation or person. When my daughters were in middle school, they used the slang phrase "Yas Queen" to describe someone who was amazing or strong or winning. Now I think of that phrase as an acronym for "yield," "accept," and "surrender," because, when we learn to do that, we become queens (or kings) of our own world. Only when we yield to reality, accept the truth of a situation, and surrender to whatever it's trying to teach us can we truly embrace the divine dance of learning and balance fate with free will.

Light Lessons: Freezing Negative Energy

This simple exercise can help you block negative energy that may be keeping you from amending your soul plan. Identify an emotional trauma from your past, a generational pattern that has kept you from using your power of choice, or a childhood experience that has kept you from moving forward. Write this down on a piece of paper and place it in a bottle of water. Put the bottle in the freezer to energetically freeze the negative power this experience has over you. Be sure to use a plastic bottle and leave a little space at the top so it won't shatter as the water freezes.

CHAPTER 8

Becoming the Hero of Your Story

Dear Soul,

You have reached the point in your studies where it is time to learn that life is not so much about what happens to you; it's about how you choose to respond to what happens to you. This is one the most difficult courses you will take while here. There will be times in your life when it feels as if you have no choices. Sometimes, when the options you do have are all terrible, you may feel as if you are stuck "between a rock and a hard place."

Yet in every moment, you are gifted with the freedom of choice. Your power lies in your ability to recognize your choices and choose well. You can choose to stay or go. You can choose to respond with kindness or cruelty. You can choose to lean on your allies or deny their help. You can choose to complain or accept a situation with grace. As you learned in the course on amending your soul plan, *you always have the power to choose a new path toward fulfilling your soul purpose.*

    You always have the power to write your own story.

YOU CAN TAKE ANYONE'S LIFE STORY AND SPIN IT IN a positive or negative direction—including your own. The power in your story lies in how you choose to see it. Joseph Campbell spent years researching myths from around the world and used them as a way to explain the choices we have to face in order to take control of our lives and turn them in a positive direction. In his book *The Hero's Journey*, he broke this journey down into a series of stages—answering the call, finding mentors, crossing the threshold, meeting challenges, entering the cave, transformation, and return. Let's explore what each of these stages means in relation to the path you choose to discover and fulfill your soul purpose.

Answering the Call

The hero's journey begins in the ordinary world in which you go about your business working, going to school, and paying bills. You live in this world until you hear the call of your soul—the call that prompts you to leave that world in search of adventure. Many choose to ignore this call, because it threatens to force them out of the comfortable ordinary life they've been living. This call often masquerades as illness, divorce, or a loss of some kind. But however it manifests, the call induces change and requires that you make choices. It calls you to leave the ordinary world to explore your true path.

CRYSTALS FOR COURAGE

- Citrine, carnelian, sunstone, yellow jade, garnet, and amazonite are all crystals that prompt and support courage. Visualize yourself radiating courage and confidence as you hold one of these crystals. Then place it outside in the sun for three to four hours. Carry it with you or place it over an affirmation like: "I am ready to answer the call of my soul."

Because you have free will, you can either accept or refuse this call. When you choose to answer the call of your soul, you are given the chance to live an uncommon life—a heroic life. If I hadn't answered the call of my own soul, I would still be teaching English at a community college. And in many ways, I'd be happy there. But there would still be this whole unexplored part of my soul yearning for something more. We all hear the call. For some, it may be a call to create art, or to write, or to play a musical instrument. It may come as a call to open your own business, or sign up for a marathon, or get that degree. However it comes, it will invite you to reach beyond the ordinary world to explore who you really are. When you leave the ordinary world, you become the hero of your own story.

When you hear the call of your soul, you feel a pull toward a spiritual life, and this can come in many ways. Some are practically slapped in the face by the Universe—a sudden job loss, an unexpected illness, or the loss of a loved one, for example. But even if you hear the call in one of these tragic ways, when you look back through the months and years before you heard it, you will find that, in those long, dark nights when sleep alluded you, your soul was always whispering to you, nudging you forward, urging you to embark on a journey out of the ordinary: "There's something more to this. There's something more to *you.*"

In literature and film, heroes often reject the call. Yet sometimes they have no choice but to answer it. When Dorothy enters the Land of Oz, she has to follow the yellow brick road. When Peter Parker is bitten by the spider, he has to become Spider Man. When Nemo is captured, Marlin must face his fears. When Rocky decides to fight Apollo Creed, he could choose to stay with his sweet girlfriend and his loyal dog. But he doesn't. He knows that the fighter inside of him has to answer. Harry Potter could have ignored his invitation to Hogwarts, but he doesn't, because he knows that there is a magical world awaiting him. And there's a magical world awaiting you now, as well.

Answering the call of your soul is the scariest thing you can do, because it means change. It means facing your fears and confronting your truth. It means choosing to leave all you know that is safe, secure, and comforting. But what happens if you refuse this call? Nothing good. You remain in the ordinary world, forever feeling a sense of loss over not having achieved your fullest potential.

I heard the call to awaken my intuition many times throughout my life, and, each time, I refused it. What would people think? Would I be labeled a weirdo? My idea of a spiritual person was someone who gave up all earthly possessions and went to a mountaintop to meditate. Yet each time I refused the call, I rejected a piece of myself.

To be a spiritual person, to answer the call of your soul, you don't have to give up your comforts or your security. You don't even have to surrender your anger. To be a spiritual person, all you have to do is embrace yourself—all of yourself—exactly as you are and where you are, and then surrender it all to your higher purpose.

When you answer the call of your soul, you embark on the greatest journey of your life—the journey within.

Finding Mentors

Along this journey, you will find many teachers and help-ers—Campell calls them "mentors." These mentors act as signposts along your life journey, pointing out hints and clues you may not have recognized when you encountered them—that teacher in middle school who said you were a great artist; that boss who said he'd never met such a natural leader; the friend who always asks you for advice because you're such a great listener.

One of the best ways to recognize these mentors is to remain open to praise. When people compliment you, do you shy away from these accolades? Who me? When someone offers you a compliment, how do you respond? Do you quickly say: "Oh this? I got it on sale. It's nothing." Or "Thank you for the praise on my presentation, but it's the team who did the work." When you respond like this, you refuse the call of your soul and push away people who may be invaluable mentors in your life.

The mentors in your life never arrive wearing nametags: "Hello. My name is Jen and I will be your teacher for this leg of your journey." In *Nemo*, Dory is a mentor, but she doesn't seem to fit the bill. Someone who suffers from short-term memory loss is probably not someone you'd pick to help you navigate a treacherous ocean voyage. Yet she's exactly what Marlin needs. Her apparent weakness becomes the strength he requires. He must forget his fears and worries, and learn to live in the present moment in order to complete his hero's journey.

In fairy tales, mentors are often fairy godmothers, although they may be disguised at first. Your mentor may be your annoying ex-wife who always pushed you to do more. Or it could be your demanding boss who pushes all your buttons. And yet out of that stress, you emerge as the hero you always were, just like a diamond forming from a lump of coal.

Crossing the Threshold

The next stage of the hero's journey is crossing the threshold. Once you've answered the call and accepted the help of your mentors, you are finally ready to leave the ordinary world and cross into the unknown. In the Tarot, this is often represented by the Tower card, which depicts two people falling from a tower as lightning strikes it. Now all your walls are down. You feel lost, vulnerable, alone, and confused. This descent is the hardest stage of the hero's journey, but it is the most important. It is here that your fears are laid bare, and you must confront your shadows and claim your innermost truths.

When you leave the ordinary world, answer the call, and descend into your soul's depths, you may feel misunderstood, lost, and alone. That's okay. This feeling is actually an illusion, because you are surrounded by unseen allies. Something magical happens when you have the courage to leave your ordinary world and seek your true destiny. The right people show up at the right time. You receive inspiration just when you're on your knees begging for help. You experience mystical dreams, insights, synchronicities, and coincidences that gently but firmly show you the way.

When I was going through my divorce, I felt alone, angry, and confused. I was angry at God. Hadn't I done everything asked of me? I had been a great wife and mother. What had I done to deserve this? One day as I sat on my deck to meditate, I found myself screaming inside my head at God. And I was shocked to hear an equally angry voice yelling back at me: "What have I taken from you? Nothing. I've woken you from the nightmare of illusions you clung to. I am Michelangelo freeing you from the stone you were trapped in. I am freeing you from the illusions you chained yourself to your whole life." I'm not claiming to be Neal Donald Walsh, nor do I hear voices in my head. But hearing those words delivered in that way at the precise moment I needed to hear them shook me free from the pity party I'd decided to throw myself. Finally, I was ready to cross the threshold into my greatest fear—being alone. And you know what I discovered? Me. Anything you fear can be your greatest teacher. Your fears are, in fact, the threshold you must cross in order to manifest the full potential of who you really are.

Meeting Challenges

Now here comes the fun part. Just when you think: "Okay, I've got this. I'm strong and confident. I'm answering that call. I'm braving the unknown. I'm facing my fears. I am a badass. Nothing can stop me now." Then boom! Something, or someone, happens to stop you. It's important to recognize and accept this stage of your spiritual awakening. It happens to all of us.

The tests and challenges thrown at you often come in the form of mean, angry people, or a sudden, unexpected loss. But just as often, they arrive as the dreaded dark night of the soul. In his book *The Ultimate Anti-Career Guide*, Rick Jarrow describes it like this: "When one door closes, another opens. But there's often a long hallway between those doors." He calls these challenges "threshold guardians," adding that they are an essential part of the journey if you want to be your authentic self.

And that's what you are here to do—be authentic. You are here to embrace and explore your mystical, magical side. It's just that, when you do this, when you stand up and claim your inner power, those stuck in the ordinary world tend to get really upset. Just by standing up for yourself, you challenge them and everything they know to be true. Quantum physics has taught us that we're all connected. Like a mobile hanging over a child's crib, if one person changes position, it affects us all. So embrace these challenges. Welcome these tests. And show the Universe that you're stronger than whatever it can throw at you.

To use a shallow example, think of a time when you went on a diet. You're in the zone. You're cutting calories; you're exercising. The pounds are coming off, and you're feeling amazing. But before you can buy those jeans one size down—bam!—you hit a plateau. No matter what you do, the scale won't budge. Many people stop there, returning to their old habits, welcomed back into the bosom of the ordinary world they left, forever wondering why life never works out for them. *Do not fall into this trap*. Recognize these challenges for what they are— the Universe knocking at your door to see if you're truly ready to be the hero of your own life.

When the Universe comes to your door with its laundry list of tests and challenges, that's the time to lean on those mentors you've welcomed into your heart. That's the time to reach within to the heart and soul of who you are and find the rich soil of desire waiting to be fertilized with your fighting spirit. Keep going. It's time to meet yourself and find out just how powerful you can be.

Entering the Cave

In the next stage, entering the cave, you must embrace your solitude. Does this mean you have to go live in a cave and meditate for the next five years? No, of course not. But it does mean that you must cast off your old persona—all those preconceived notions about who you thought you were, and all the expectations placed on you by others. This is when you learn who you are without all the labels you thought defined you. This is the part of your spiritual journey when you're asked to shed those preconceptions—to peel them away like the layers of an onion until you get to the authentic core of your being.

When I was a teacher, I always told my students that everything can be taken from us—money, jobs, homes, health—but you can never lose your education. As I watched my father struggle with the final stages of Alzheimer's, however, I realized that even this could be taken from us. Yet even though my dad couldn't remember my name, his kindness—that innate quality that had always defined him—was still there. Every day, he hugged me and said: "You're a good one. You're a good person. Never forget that." Watching my dad fade away from me in inches made me realize that, when you stripped away all his labels—award-winning advertising executive, father, husband, and friend with thirty-five years of sobriety to his credit—what you found beneath them was a kind soul.

This is the stage of your journey where you are forced to strip away all the illusions you've been clinging to, all the labels that have been slapped on you. This is when you discover who you really are. This poem by first-century poet Izumi Shikibu—one of my favorites—illustrates this stage of the journey perfectly.

> *Watching the moon*
> *at dawn,*
> *solitary, mid-sky,*
> *I knew myself completely:*
> *no part left out.*

It's in the solitary, metaphorical cave of self-reflection that you are finally able to know who you are, what you're capable of doing, and why you're here in this school called Earth. This is a crucial step in learning the divine dance of the Universe, because it leads you to take action to achieve your dreams and goals. This is the "walking your talk" part of the journey that leads to transformation.

Transformation

Now you must step into the ring and show the world what you're made of. Even when you have overcome challenges, embraced the help of your mentors, and faced your innermost fears, there always comes a time when you have to step up and into your light. Harry Potter knew he had Ron and Hermione behind him and the wisdom of Dumbledore to guide him, but he had to face Voldemort on his own. When Simba finally dealt with his guilt over his father's death in *The Lion King* and was ready to reclaim Pride Rock, he had to do it alone. This is the stage of your soul's journey when you must step up and show the world what you're made of.

If the artist within you has finally awakened, this is when you have to put your work on display for all to see. If your dream is to own your own business, this is when you have to hang that "Open" sign on the door and present yourself to customers. If your journey so far has been about learning to stand up for yourself, this is when you must face your nemesis and be heard, seen, and validated. You may feel scared, unsure, and alone, but that's okay. Do it anyway. You may feel like an imposter, unworthy, or foolish. That's okay. Do it anyway. It is only when you stand in your truth and shine your light that you are fully in communion with your soul.

I've done a lot of scary things in my life. I spent a year teaching teenagers who had just been released from prison. I went diving with sharks. I faced a terrifying health diagnosis. But the scariest thing I've ever done is to answer the call of my soul. When I came out of the psychic closet, I was sure I would lose all my friends, that my family would freak out, that I'd lose my job, that I'd never be seen as normal again. But then a thought hit me. I'd been trying my whole life to fit in. And then I thought about that phrase and what it implied—being forced into a mold that someone else created. To meet the challenges on your journey and be willing to enter the cave of your inner-most self is to break out of that confining mold and fly free. This is where you transform into who you truly are.

Like the Ugly Duckling who discovers it's a swan, nothing has changed, yet everything is different. During your transformation, you realize that *everything* is good—all the bad things that have happened to you, all the challenges and tests you've faced, all the doubts and inner worries you've confronted—are all good, because they've led you to the point of transformation. Rather than transforming into someone different, what's really happened is that you've shed the skin of your illusions and revealed what had been hidden inside all along—*you*.

Roman mythology tells us that, when people petitioned Fortuna, the goddess of good luck and fortune, she held back her blessing, waiting to see if they took the first step toward their goal on their own. Only when they called on their own resources to arrive on the threshold of success did she intercede and offer them assistance. And this is how the Universe works for us as well. Only when we have shed our illusions and embraced our true selves can we experience a revelation of perfect understanding.

Return

Knowing without question who you are and why you're here is the most beautiful gift you can aspire to receive. When your truth is revealed, you no longer experience moments of profound doubt and worry. You know yourself. You know what you have to offer. You accept your soul purpose, and you are ready to return to the ordinary world and share it with others.

This has always been hard for me, because I'm comfortable with doubting myself. If the world handed out medals for best doubter, I would win the gold. I could never quite see what I had to offer the world that wasn't already out there. Even the Bible tells us that there's nothing new under the sun. What could I possibly contribute to the world that would be of value?

Then something dancer Martha Graham said helped me realize that we each have a unique gift to share with the world:

> There is a vitality, a life force, an energy, a quickening that is translated through you into action, and because there is only one of you in all of time, this expression is unique. And if you block it, it will never exist through

any other medium, and it will be lost. The world will not have it. It is not your business to determine how good it is nor how valuable nor how it compares with other expressions. It is your business to keep it yours clearly and directly, to keep the channel open. You do not even have to believe in yourself or your work. You have to keep yourself open and aware to the urges that motivate you.

Reread Graham's words and take a moment to reflect on your unique self and what it has to offer the Universe.

Something is waiting to be born inside each of us. When you are open to receiving, you let the light in, you invite inspiration to dance with you, and you give birth to your true purpose. When you return to the ordinary world at the end of your hero's journey, you realize that you are spirit, and you rise to take your place in the light. You prepare yourself to help others on their journey. When you answer the call of your soul, you learn that fate is what happens to you, but destiny is what you do about it.

Light Lessons: Meeting Your Future Self

Time is not linear. Your future self exists now. But you can alter and affect your future through meditation, intent, and sustained thought. This exercise can help you connect with your future self to learn what you need to know to get where you want to be. Try reading this meditation into a recording device and playing it back to yourself as you sit in quiet reflection.

For this exercise, you will need a pen or pencil, some paper, and a crystal for focus, like clear quartz, lapis lazuli, amethyst, or citrine.

Sit comfortably in a meditation position. Take several deep breaths. Imagine a ball of white light coming through your body, beginning at your crown chakra. See this ball of light coming in through the top of your head and descending through your body, illuminating each chakra as it travels down. Breathe this calming, healing light into your bones, cells, and tissues. Breathe it down through your knees, calves, and feet. See it resting beneath your feet, lighting up your whole body.

Imagine yourself in your meditative space—by the ocean, in a crystal cave, in a lush forest or a meadow. The more clearly you can imagine this, the more easily you'll move into the theta state needed for meditation. Take some time getting comfortable there.

You notice something unusual in your meditation space—something that appears in your peripheral vision. As you turn to face it, you see a time machine with its door standing open. You feel called to this time machine and walk over to it. As you slip inside, you find a cylindrical calendar. You turn the wheels to adjust it until it shows this exact date, but five years in the future.

You feel the machine vibrate and hum to life and see yourself going through a tunnel. At first it glows with a red light, then the light turns to orange, then yellow, then green, then light blue. The colors rush through you. The tunnel now glows in a wondrous shade of indigo, then a vibrant purple. As you slow down, it settles into a brilliant white light. The machine stops and the door opens.

As you get out, you find yourself in a white room with two chairs. Your future self is seated in one of them. Walk toward your future self and take a moment to ask what you need to know about your future life. Are you happy? Where are you working? What important relationships are there in your life? What relationships have left your life and how did this affect you? What are you worried about? What can you do now, in the present, to help yourself in the future?

Finally, ask your future self if there is anything else you need to know, and how often you should come back to check in with the future you.

When you are done, flutter your eyes open and write down the answers you received with your non-dominant hand. When you write with this hand, it allows your subconscious and intuition to flow more smoothly. When you are done writing down everything you remember, take a walk and use this time to process the important information you just received.

CHAPTER 9

Creating the Life You Want

Dear Soul,

While you're attending the University of Earth, you will be told that everything you need exists outside of you. This is simply not true. All you need to graduate from this challenging school is already inside of you. Learn how to utilize the power of your words, your thoughts, your intentions, and your imagination to become the beautiful co-creator you already are.

WE HAVE FOUR POWERFUL TOOLS AT OUR DISPOSAL as we journey through the school of life—our words, our thoughts, our intentions, and our imaginations. When you use these tools correctly, you can manifest the life of your dreams and embrace your ability to create opportunities, even miracles, in your life. You are a co-creator with the Universe. The moment you accept that fact, you will start to feel more empowered to manifest changes in your life. You may feel powerless to change the circumstances life hands you. But in reality, you are the captain of your ship and you can direct the course of your life.

The Power of Words

All of creation starts with our words, which have their roots in our thoughts and intentions. Our words hold immense power. In fact, the Bible tells us that God created the world through the Word, or *logos*, and teaches that "the tongue has the power of life and death" (Proverbs 18:21). Catholics pray aloud to petition for healing, salvation, and inner peace. Pagans use the power of words in healing rituals. The Torah enumerates eleven sins that are committed through words. Tibetans believe that a powerful sound, *Om*, began all creation and use mantras to heal and bring about enlightenment. Solomon Islanders believe they can fell trees by screaming insults at their spirits for thirty days. Words create history. Americans declared their freedom and then put those words into action. Todd Beamer's words "Let's roll" helped save thousands of lives.

New research shows that words and sounds can physically heal our bodies. Mother Theresa reminded us that the echoes of the words we speak are "truly endless." Words entertain us, teach us, empower us, and instruct us. We use them to communicate our thoughts and intentions. We use them to make vows, negotiate contracts, and seal partnerships. With our words, we swear oaths, declare freedom, and create our reality.

Words, when spoken, become vibrations that affect the energy around you. Thus you can use them to create change, open up opportunities, and effect healing. You create your own mood every day with your words. When you wake up tomorrow, try saying aloud: "I feel great" or "Today is going to be a fantastic day." Then notice how these words affect your mood.

In *Love As a Way of Life*, Gary Chapman describes words as either bullets or seeds, and endows them with the power to either create or destroy. Jean Paul Sartre called them "loaded pistols." Florence Scovel Shinn and Louise Hay claim that the words we speak create our destiny and call spoken affirmations "prescriptions," because they have the power to heal physically and emotionally.

Every day, you have a choice as to how you will use your words. When you speak your truth, your desires, and your wishes aloud, you affirm and declare your right to claim the outcome of those words. You can choose to use words as seeds to grow the life you want, or as bullets to kill your happiness. You can use them as a means to turn your dreams into reality, or as weapons to take down others or destroy your own self-esteem. When you embrace the power of your words to create the life you're meant to live, you are guided to fulfilling your life's purpose, and are automatically happier.

The Power of Thoughts

We've all heard the expression: "Thoughts are things." And science has proven this. Thoughts can be measured electro-magnetically. The protein bases of DNA look like the syntax of a genetic language, which has led scientists to speculate that our words may truly influence our DNA.

TIP FOR MANIFESTING WITH CRYSTALS

• Write your goal on a piece of paper. Fold it toward you to invite the energy of your goal into your life. Place it under a plant like bamboo or jade, then press a green aventurine, moss agate, or green jade into the soil of the plant to remind you that, as this plant grows, your goal also grows closer to completion.

As one Chinese proverb tells us: "Thought is the ancestor of action." When you harness the power of your thoughts, you become a co-creator of the world around you. Every thought is alive once you give birth to it. Once you stop thinking a thought, however, it recedes and becomes inactive. The only things that stay alive and active and working for you are those to which you give your attention. Take a minute to really reflect on this. Your thoughts are constantly creating your reality.

In a fascinating experiment, psychologist Ellen Langer illustrated the power of our inner thoughts, showing how they could be influenced by the placebo effect. Her goal was to determine if our perception of how much we exercise could affect our physical bodies. The study population consisted of eighty-four hotel maids. When asked about their level of exercise, the majority of these women responded that they didn't believe they were getting enough exercise, despite the physically demanding nature of their jobs. Langer and her team measured the women's body weight, blood pressure, and body fat. Then they divided them into two groups. The first group was informed of how many calories they were burning as they performed their tasks. The second was given no information on calorie burn. At the end of the experiment, members of the first group were told that they were more than meeting the daily requirements for fitness and exercise.

A month later, Langer and her team re-evaluated the women. The first group—those who were told that their daily tasks were helping them burn significant calories and stay in shape—showed a significant drop in blood pressure, weight, and percentage of body fat. The second group—those who were not told anything—exhibited no significant change in their weight or blood pressure. Neither of these two groups had changed one thing about their daily work routine. Apparently, if you believe you're exercising and working on fitness, your body responds accordingly. This is how powerful your thoughts can be.

So how can you train your mind to think thoughts that will positively impact your life? It all starts with understanding the potent power of your subconscious mind and the unique way in which it works.

The subconscious mind is literal. If you tell yourself you will be wealthy one day, that is what your mind will give you in return—the hope that one day you will be wealthy. If you tell it you want more money, that's what it will give you—the desire, the ambition, for more money. If you tell it that you *need* money, however, that is what the Universe will give you—the need for more money. So if what you want is financial security, instead say: "I have all the money I need now to pay my bills, shop with ease, invest in the stock market, and save for retirement."

The subconscious mind responds only to positive words. Try saying to yourself: "Don't picture a pink elephant." What's the first thing you see in your mind? A pink elephant, right? If you tell yourself you're not in debt, your subconcious ignores the negative word and hears: "I am in debt." So if you want a healthy cash flow, instead say: "I pay my bills with ease."

Today, science is helping prove the power of our thoughts to create the life around us. They have identified a bundle of nerves at the base of the skull called the "reticular activating system," or RAS. These nerves have several functions, including the ability to filter out data. This system acts like a gatekeeper or a bouncer at a loud, crowded bar. It decides what information gets into your brain and subconscious and what information, events, and experiences are kept out.

Your RAS looks for situations that will validate and prove your beliefs, and filters out information that doesn't fit within your spectrum of convictions. If you think that people are mean, the RAS acts like a robot that is programmed to seek out people who are mean to help you validate and affirm this belief. But if you think your life is easy and fun, it will work hard to deliver events, people, and experiences that prove that your life is easy and fun. So when you repeat a daily affirmation that focuses your mind on a specific thought, you program your RAS to create that reality for you.

Your RAS also filters out irrelevant data so that you see and hear only what you expect to. Think of a time you were in a crowded space—a bar, a sporting event, a concert—and still somehow managed to hear your name being called. How is it that you can be in such a noisy environment and still hear your name called? That happens because your RAS filters out all the extraneous noise to deliver only what you need to hear. Or perhaps you purchased a turquoise van and suddenly you see turquoise vans everywhere. That's your RAS filtering out irrelevant information and helping you see the things you expect to see.

There can be up to a billion bits of data coming to you at any one time, but your brain can only process so much. That's why the RAS only allows certain information to come through. But how does it know what to let in? It judges by the thoughts and impressions on which you focus. So if you think that you are clumsy, you invite or only notice circumstances in which you're clumsy. That's why people who say they are always broke tend to have persistent money issues. Look for and notice the times when you think thoughts that begin with phrases like "I always" or "I never." Pay attention to how you formulate thoughts that begin with "I am," because they can have a powerful effect on the RAS. Your thoughts lead to belief, which in turn leads the RAS to deliver proof of your beliefs.

But the good news is that you can program your RAS by telling it what to look for. The RAS can't guess or figure out what you want. It pays attention only to the thoughts and impressions on which you focus. When you constantly dwell on how awful your job is or how lonely you are, you tell your RAS to find and deliver events that prove these beliefs to be true.

And this applies to everything you feed your brain. When all you watch on TV is the news, or reality shows in which people are constantly fighting, or violent crime shows, you program your RAS to deliver information that shows you that life is hard and people are mean. This doesn't mean that you can't watch these shows or keep up with the news, but it does mean you should be aware of what you're feeding your mind. Keep your viewing in balance. Watch the news, then turn to an uplifting show or read a happy, positive book on spirituality.

If you start to think that you are good with money, your RAS will respond by only showing you events in which you're good with money. If you believe that people love you or that success always finds you, this is what you'll start to notice in your life. Think about this for a moment. Or for the rest of your life. That's how important this is. If your RAS can filter out noise, chaos, and pounding music to help you hear your name being called across a crowded room, then it can also filter out the chaos of negativity and help you focus on the positive things you want to invite into your life.

So how can you make this work for you? Studies show you have to repeat an affirming thought 100 times a day to program your RAS. Think about something you want to see more of in your life or a negative habit you want to turn into a positive one. Write it down in an "I am" statement, for instance: "I am healthy, happy, loved, and loving." Then repeat this thought 100 times throughout your day. Before you know it, you'll start seeing your life shift in amazing and seemingly magical ways.

Your thoughts are powerful tools for change, manifesting, healing, and growth. What you think about on a daily basis finds meaning in what you perceive and creates your attitude about your life. In today's world, you are mired in nonstop distractions in your everyday life. Your phone beeps and rings and buzzes at you. Emails and texts demand your attention, and countless hours of streaming entertainment clutter your thoughts, making it hard to pause and focus on what you really want and need in order to thrive and feel connected to your soul purpose.

But when you allow yourself to be distracted in this way, you give the world around you permission to tell you who you are and how you should feel. You let the outside world decide for you what is meaningful and what isn't. If you think of attention and intention as a form of currency, then you're being robbed all the time.

The best practice for developing control of your thoughts is mindful meditation. It opens a space in which subtle perceptions can arise by teaching you to make friends with boredom. It helps you to become intimately acquainted with your own mind. The easiest way to focus your thoughts is to still your mind and quietly go within, so you can listen to your heart. And that's what empowers your intentions.

The Power of Intentions

Intentions are simply goals married to determination. Together, these project a powerful force out into the world. Many people go through life allowing circumstances to happen to them, rather than cultivating the power of their own thoughts and intentions to create the circumstances they want to experience. Every thought emits a powerful vibration, so imagine what a powerful, positive thought aligned with your focused determination can create for you.

You are a co-creator of your world. The moment you realize this, you begin to feel more empowered to manifest changes and create opportunities in your life. You may feel powerless in the face of the circumstances life hands you. But in reality, you can direct the course of your life through your intentions.

Your life, your reality, is simply the story you repeatedly tell yourself. Think carefully about the story you tell about your own life. Do you focus on your difficult childhood? Your parents' divorce? Constantly moving from one place to another? Feeling stuck in the same small town? Do you ruminate over others who were cruel to you at school? Or are you constantly reliving the "good ole days," feeling as if they are forever in your rear-view mirror? Do you often lie in bed at night reliving past regrets and perceived failures?

Try allowing yourself to think instead about the wonders of the real you—your successes, your ability to get back up after a defeat or loss, the strength you've earned and learned from the difficult times. Do you ever celebrate your ability to get back in there and fight the good fight? Or your talent for making people laugh and relax and just feel better about themselves? The more you can focus your energy on the positive aspects of your life story, the healthier you will be, and the more easily you will manifest your dreams and goals.

We all carry pain from the past. But when you keep reliving that pain or choose to let those hard memories to define you, you allow it to become your story. Because what you focus on is what you create, this simply leads you to create more opportunities for pain.

Science has proven that we all emit an energy field. Sometimes we can even see these fields, and we can always feel them. Have you ever been around someone who is so confident and full of energy that you just instinctively feel that you have to stand up a little straighter and work to rise up to that higher energy level? Or have you ever been around a friend who's so downtrodden that you tend to shrink a little so you can commiserate and offer sympathy? Take a moment to think about your own energy field. What energy do you emit on an average day? Are your vibrations high or low on the scale? Remember: Like attracts like. That's a universal law. So it follows that you are always attracted to people who are like you. If you continually focus on rewriting your life story as a tragedy, you will attract more tragic events and people into your energy field.

Years ago, when I was going through several difficult months, I decided to meditate and ask my spirit guide to help me raise my negative energy and move into a higher vibration. My guide showed me an old video store—this was before the days of streaming video—that was divided into sections: comedy, romance, drama, horror, action, thrillers, mystery, and adventure. I saw an image of myself standing in front of the drama section. Then I heard my guide say: "You can always choose the section where you want to live and experience life. Stop allowing yourself to be guided to the wrong vibration. Life doesn't have to be a drama, unless you allow it to be so." In the meditation, I saw myself consciously moving to the comedy section. This was a really profound message for me—one I've often thought of through the years. What section of the video store are you living in now? Which one do you want to live in?

You are not the sole author of your life story, however. God is your co-writer, as are others who come along and add to your narrative. Some write wonderful chapters; others leave episodes you may want to tear out and rewrite. But that's life. Your job is to take up the pen and edit and amend your story, removing what you don't want there and adding what you want included. Once you realize that you have this ability, this power, anything—even manifesting your goals—becomes truly possible.

Start with small intentions like: "Today will be a great day." Or "I intend to have a successful week at work." Then gradually move on to bigger intentions. Focus on where you want to be in one year, then five years. Write it down and make it happen. Powerful energies shift within you when you speak your thoughts and intentions aloud and then write them down.

One of the best ways to align with your intentions and use the power of your words and thoughts is to create a goal book. I've been doing this for years and have used mine to manifest jobs, salary increases, pregnancies, vacations, even love. Each new year, write down three to five goals you want to achieve in the next twelve months. Write these as positive affirmations in the present tense. Then flip through magazines and cut out pictures that represent these goals and glue them below your affirmations. If one of your goals is to find love or strengthen an existing partnership, you can write: "My relationship is loving, respectful, balanced, healthy, passionate, and fun." Then glue a picture of a couple holding hands below your statement. For a financial goal, you can cut out pictures of money or tape a bill on the page and write "paid in full" over it. Then place the pages in a binder or attach them together using a paperclip or a stapler.

Keep your goal book by your bedside and look at it every night before you go to sleep for at least twenty-one, but no more than forty, days. Studies have shown that, when you do something consistently for three weeks, your brain acclimates to this new way of thinking and acting. Visualize yourself achieving all your desires and imagine the feeling that goes along with that achievement. This activates the law of attraction and makes you a magnet for the ideas, opportunities, and synchronicities that need to occur to bring your dreams to fruition. Each time I create a goal book, I also create a playlist of uplifting music. I listen to the playlist every day as I run errands or clean the house or walk the dogs, while imagining my goals coming true.

Whenever you feel worried or anxious that a goal has not yet been achieved, or because you're not really sure it will happen, record that worry or fear on a separate page. Then rip up the page and throw it away. This forces you to face your fears and worries and release them from your energy. Don't get discouraged if you have negative thoughts or try to ignore them. Just replace them with positive thoughts, which are much more powerful than negative thoughts.

Have fun with this and be creative. One student created a goal book based on the chakras—financial goals on a red page for the root chakra; creative goals on an orange page for the sacral chakra; relationship goals on a green page for the heart chakra. Some draw their own pictures, while some create beautiful pages decorated with stickers. Or you can create something simple with just a glue stick and a few pieces of paper. The key is to remain open to the different ways your goals may materialize for you. On the last page, write: "This or something better. For the good of all. Thank you!"

When the twenty-one to forty days have passed, put your goal book in a drawer and release it to the Universe, knowing that all your goals will manifest and materialize for you. Remember, this is all about intention. Every time you create a goal book, you tell the Universe: "This is how I intend my life to be." Be open to all your goals manifesting in ways you may never have imagined or planned, and have faith that they will materialize. The most important thing is to have fun and trust the Universe, knowing that your intentions will all be realized.

The Power of Positive Thinking

There is great power in thinking consistently positive thoughts that feed your soul with the love and encouragement it deserves. But to do this, you have to work

22259

on keeping your energetic vibrations up. And this means maintaining an attitude of hopeful expectation and a positive mindset. It's crucial that you start to observe how certain situations, thoughts, people, and habits bring you down so that you can avoid them—or at least minimize your exposure to them. You probably can't be positive and upbeat every minute of every day, but there are some things you can do each day to help boost your positive vibes and keep your energy at a higher level so you can maintain consistently positive thoughts. Here are just a few:

- Take a break from negative news. The world won't end if you aren't up-to-date on every current event.
- Get outside for at least ten minutes each day. Take a walk, go for a bike ride, walk your dog, or just sit in your yard in the sunshine.
- Drink lots of water to help flush toxins out of your body and keep you energized and energetically clear.
- Get plenty of sleep. Try going to bed at least thirty minutes earlier than you normally do.
- Start the day with something that makes you happy to set the tone for the whole day. Do yoga stretches, say a prayer, read poetry or something introspective, write in your journal, take a morning walk, or watch an uplifting show.
- Wear or carry a crystal that can raise your vibrations, like clear quartz, sunstone, golden healer, citrine, pink opal, or rose quartz.

- Place a big jar in your kitchen and, each day for a week, jot down one (or two or three) things for which you're grateful. At the end of the week, read through them and consider how fortunate you really are. Or you can do this at the start of each new year. Then, on the following New Year's Eve, read through them to remind yourself of all the good things in your life.

- Create a playlist that's filled with happy, uplifting music. Listen to it often. Dance to it.

- Eat salads, raw veggies, and fruit each day.

- Take a weekly salt bath to scrub your energetic field clean. Just pour a cup of Epsom Salts and ½ cup of sea salt into your bath and soak for at least twenty minutes. Or rub this mixture all over your skin in the shower as you visualize all your negativity going down the drain.

- Take just five or ten minutes each day to stop, slow down, and tune in to what's good in your life. Listen to a guided meditation or just sit in a relaxed position while focusing on your breathing or a positive affirmation.

- Do something creative just for fun. Bake cookies, play with clay, paint, write, or draw.

- Walk around barefoot to help you feel more connected to the Earth and ground your energy. This will calm and center you.

- Commit to your own happiness by doing something just for you—get a manicure, go out to dinner, buy something you've been wanting, say "no" to something you don't want to do, plan a vacation.
- Enjoy a thirty-second hug. Studies show that when you receive a hug that lasts thirty seconds, all sorts of wonderful endorphins fire off in your body.
- Clean and declutter your home or office; buy a plant to raise the vibrations of your home; perform a random act of kindness for someone.
- Each day for a week, take a picture of three things or people that made you happy that day. Look through these images at the end of the week to relive that happy feeling.
- Give back to someone who helped increase your positive vibes. Did a babysitter save the day for you this week? Get her a gift certificate to her favorite store. Did a co-worker make you laugh after a bad day? Take him out to lunch. Did your neighbor take your garbage bins out when you forgot? Bake some muffins to say thank you.

The Power of Imagination

In order to use the power of your thoughts and intentions, you have to take action steps like those given above to maintain a positive atitiude. And even more important, you must work with the power of your imagination. You can do this through meditation, visualization, and daydreams.

When you make time each day to give your imagination free reign and daydream, it keeps your mind sharp and helps you turn your goals and dreams into reality. One recent study showed that people who daydream are smarter than their more-focused peers. Scientists have also shown that the brain processes daydreams in the same way it processes memories. This means that your subconscious stores your daydreams as facts. And once you get an idea or a belief into your subconscious, you can bring it from the dream state into real time.

The subconscious mind is tricky, however. You have no control over what gets stored there. It's designed to protect you, which means that you tend to store things there that are charged with strong emotions—the highs and lows of your life, memories that are rooted in strong emotions like fear or joy. But metaphysics has shown that you can change the inner programming of your subconscious through repeated affirmations, although this takes a lot of time. The problem has always been getting your subconscious mind on board with your intentions and goals in a timely manner.

Moreover, sometimes when you try to "retrain your brain," you end up reenforcing limiting beliefs and self-sabotaging thoughts, because the subconscious is where you tend to store the negative messages you received as a child: "You can't make a living as an artist." Or "You're not smart enough for that degree." How many times have you started a new year with great resolutions and then stopped a month or two later because you hit a road-block or two? Your subconscious mind loves to tell you what you can't do by playing and replaying old thoughts and old memories of past "failures." But when you replace these old memories with positive future memories in the form of daydreams and affirmations, you remove these subconscious blocks.

Most often, we reach the subconscious by accessing the theta and alpha brain states through deep, serious, and consistent meditation. But now science is showing that it can also be accessed through the simple act of imagining while we daydream. Daydreaming activates an area of the brain called the "default mode network," or DMN. You aren't even consciously aware of this happening and you can't control when the DMN is activated. But you *can* control the thoughts and daydreams you have in order to program it with positive images and any goals you're pursuing.

The DMN is where you get your sense of self. How can you become a co-creator with the Universe if you don't first understand yourself as the source? Most people spend about 30 percent of their day lost in thought. Unfortunately, much of this time is spent on pointless

thoughts, worries, and anxieties. But when you daydream as a focused action, you establish a direct connection to the subconscious, which is where true change and
creation occur.

Imagining your future life through daydreaming
allows you to find solutions to problems and creative
insights that otherwise might not be available to you.
The subconscious does not speak in words. It speaks
through emotion and pictures. Nor can it distinguish
between reality and fantasy, or between past, present,
and future. To the subconscious mind, everything is real
and everything is *now*. When you daydream, you program it to create the reality you're envisioning in the daydream. When your daydreams are augmented with the
emotions you would feel if these goals came true, you
really fire up the power of the subconscious mind.

What you imagine most frequently is what you create.
You are manifesting all the time. The only problem is
that when you are caught up in worries and fears, this is
what you manifest, rather than the positive life for which
you're striving. But when you learn to harness this power
and fill it with positive images and emotions, you can
jump off the continual roller coaster of positive and negative experiences and create the life you want to lead.

The key to daydreaming is to keep your daydreams
simple. Remember, your goal is to project an image into
the Universe. The more details you introduce into it, the

more weighted down your dream will be as it takes flight to the collective unconscious. Think about what you want to invite into your life. Envision yourself manifesting your goals at work, in your finances, with your health, your relationships, and your personal wishes. Feed these thoughts with the positive emotions of joy, anticipation, and excitement. When you invoke the power of your imagination through visualization and daydreaming, then add the potent force of your emotions and inspired feelings, you become an alchemist who turns dross into gold to effect positive changes in your life.

Athletes have long used the power of their imaginations to achieve success in their field. Science has shown that, when they visualize their own performance, their muscles react as if they're physically performing. One study showed that the brain patterns of weightlifters who imagined they were lifting hundreds of pounds were the same as when they actually lifted the weight. Similarly, Nathan Sharansky, a computer specialist who spent nine years in a Russian prison after being accused of spying, used his time in solitary confinement to play chess with himself, with goal of becoming the best player in the world. When he was released, he achieved that goal by beating the current world champion.

Another study showed that, while people who went to the gym increased their muscle mass by 30 percent, those who just stayed at home and visualized going to the gym increased their muscle mass by 14 percent. Likewise Roger Bannister, the runner who first broke the four-minute mile, achieved that long-elusive goal by visualizing himself achieving it. When asked how he had managed to do it, Bannister said that it all started in his mind. He had to see it there first before he could achieve it in the physical world. Through the power of his imagination and his refusal to allow negative thinking to slow him down, he achieved the goal he had set for himself. Moreover, once that four-minute barrier was broken, other runners broke it again and again because they could now see it as a possibility.

What are the four-minute barriers in your world? What beliefs are causing you to cave in and relinquish your goals? What would your life look like if you took the time to imagine the success, love, and health you deserve?

One way to harness the power of your imagination is to closely monitor and direct the way you speak to your inner self. As the poet Hafiz reminds us: "The words you speak become the house you live in." When you channel your inner speech—the way you talk to yourself and think about yourself—into positive paths, this creates a beautiful energy that facilitates healing, growth, peace, and abundance.

Try writing down three things you love about yourself every day for a week. Each morning or evening, get out your journal and give yourself three compliments.

These can be physical compliments, or emotional attributes, like your love of animals. They can be compassonate actions you have taken, like cheering up a friend or checking on a neighbor who just had surgery. They can be spiritual strengths, like your connection to spirit or your commitment to daily meditation. They can even be practical compliments: "I love the way I handled my angry boss today." Or "I'm proud of how I openly communicated my concerns to my son's teacher."

At the end of the week, read over your compliments to yourself and reflect on how this makes you feel. Did it feel awkward to compliment yourself? Did it get easier as the week went on? Was it hard to focus on yourself in such a positive light? Did you struggle to come up with three things each day, or did you have a hard time limiting yourself to just three compliments? What positive effect would it have on your life if you continued this practice on a regular basis?

Light Lessons: Year of Action

Around the time of the new year and your birthday, a powerful energy for potential surrounds you that you can use to create and shape the coming year in your own image. It's as if the Universe pauses on your doorstep to ask: "What do you want to create now? Where should you focus your intentions for the year?" You can manifest great changes and goals in your life during this period.

To begin this exercise, choose a word—one word—that defines your goals for the coming year. Decide what type of experiences you want to invite into your life. Do you want to have more fun? Do you want to work on your spirituality? Is it time to focus on your career? What about your intuitive life? Would you like to focus on love and relationships? Are you going back to school or starting new projects? Do you want to focus on health this year? Brainstorm some positive adjectives that describe you in this new year—happy, healthy, loving, forgiving, balanced. Consider activities you want to engage in during the year—travel, love, a new job, increased income, adventure, quality time with family.

Once you have your list, look it over and write down one word that captures the essence of the year you're imagining for yourself. This one word helps you to focus your thoughts and manifest your goals and hopes into reality. Then write down some actions you can take to start living into this one word. For example, if your word is "healthy," write down actions like joining a gym, working with a trainer, giving up soft drinks, or reducing sugar. If your word is "healed," write down actions like working with a life coach, connecting with a therapist, taking a meditation class, or joining a yoga group. Dislay this word somewhere where you'll see it each day—for instance, on your desk or by your bedside.

Each week throughout the year, reflect on how you're moving into your word. This process may not be easy, because the Universe likes to test us. This is just a way for you to stop and ask yourself: "Is this really what I want?" For example, let's say you picked the word "forgive" because you want to forgive your father for abandoning your family. But as you start to move into the energy of this word, you get blocked and feel frustrated. This may be the Universe's way of telling you that you're not ready for this word—and that's okay. Or it may be your guides and angels telling you that you need to ask for some help. Either way, look at any challenges or blocks you experience as opportunities to take a time-out and evaluate your process. Then you can either continue with the word or choose a new one. The purpose of this exercise is to focus your year on a specific goal so that you can direct your life down a path that fulfills you.

CHAPTER 10

The Secret Language
of the Universe

Dear Soul,

As you near the end of your studies at the University of Earth, remember that you have many tools at your disposal. In addition to your team of allies, you also have resources that enable you to connect to your spirit within. When used properly, these tools can help you recall your soul purpose, recognize present blocks, and amend your soul plan if necessary. And most important, they can help you recognize and listen to the secret language of the Universe.

When in doubt or feeling lost, dear soul, always look within. All you need for a successful life journey already resides in your authentic self.

THERE'S AN OLD STORY ABOUT A FARMER WHOSE horse ran away. His neighbors came around that evening to sympathize, saying: "That's too bad." And the farmer replied: "Maybe." The next day, when the horse came back bringing seven wild horses with him, the neighbors gathered around the farmer, exclaiming: "That's great, isn't it?" But the farmer just answered: "Maybe." On the third day, when his son broke his leg trying to tame one of the wild horses, the neighbors all commiserated with the farmer, observing: "Well that's bad luck, isn't it?" Again, the farmer answered: "Maybe." On the fourth day, when soldiers came to the farm to recruit the son for the army but rejected him because of his broken leg, all the neighbors congratulated the farmer, crying: "Well, isn't that wonderful?" To which he replied: "Maybe."

This story demonstrates clearly that there are many times in life when we can't be certain why "bad luck" has befallen us, or why "good luck" has decided to shine its bountiful light on us. A possible bad situation can turn into a beautiful opportunity; but just as often, what looks like good luck can lead to a disastrous outcome. And this uncertainty can leave us feeling as if we're pawns in this game called life.

But when you choose to see your life as an opportunity to grow and learn, this feeling of powerlessness shifts into one of limitless potential. So stop asking: "Why is this happening to me?" Ask yourself instead: "What is this trying to teach me?" And the key to understanding the answer to that question is learning the secret language of the Universe, which is always communicating with you, guiding you, and encouraging you to find your way.

Because the collective energy of the Universe isn't human, it doesn't "speak" as we do. Instead, it communicates through signs, symbols, and synchronicities. It's your job to become fluent in that language.

Signs from the Universe

Signs from the Universe can be subtle, blatant, and often humorous. A few years ago, I had been asking the Universe for a sign to help me make an important decision regarding a work opportunity. When I ask for a sign, I like to phrase it as a "yes" or "no" question accompanied by a time frame so I'll know for sure it's a sign for me. This time I prayed: "In the next three days, please show me a red cardinal for "no" or a bluebird for "yes" so I can make the best decision regarding this work opportunity."

Two days passed and I saw neither a cardinal nor a bluebird. On the third day, I was feeling a bit frustrated as I drove to pick up my children at school, so I said aloud in the car: "I'm not asking you to part the Red Sea. I'm just looking for a little guidance about this big work decision." Almost instantly, a truck pulled out in front of me bearing the name of its business—*A Sign From Above*. I laughed, realizing that the Universe is always trying to communicate with me, but this time, the answer was that I had to make this decision on my own.

When you're on the right path, these signs come quickly and clearly. When I was trying to decide how to formulate this book, I was driving to the post office when the entire structure of the book was seemingly downloaded into my consciousness. I knew I had to write this almost as a syllabus for a course of study—a manual for being a student at the University of Earth. The idea seemed too big and almost grandiose, but I couldn't shake the feeling that it seemed right. As I waited in line at the post office, I asked the Universe to show me a hawk if this was the right way to format the book. As I walked to my car, a hawk flew so low in front of me that I could see the brown-and-white pattern on its outstretched wings.

You can also ask the Universe for signs that simply bring you encouragement when you're going through a difficult time. These signs from above can help you feel less alone and remind you that, even when you're going through a difficult life lesson, the Universe always has your back, as this listener's story demonstrates so beautifully.

Recently, I received some bad career news—or rather, a disappointing lack of career news. I decided to ask the Universe for a sign that everything would turn out alright. I thought of asking for a butterfly, but I ask for those a lot, so I decided to ask for a caterpillar instead. I glumly got ready for work. When I got on the subway. I was distracted by all the things we get distracted by. But, at one point in my commute, I looked up, and there, at the top of the subway car, was a poster with a drawing of a caterpillar on it. Tears came to my eyes. Then, just as I got up to the sidewalk from the depths of the subway, a song came up on my playlist called "The Keep Going Song." I felt the song pertained to my present struggle and knew that the Universe was telling me that all would eventually work out.

It's important to ask for your own sign from the Universe for a specific request. Otherwise, you may think that every hawk, every caterpillar, or every dime you find is a sign just for you. When you have a need for clarification, hope, or a glimpse of a "yes" or "no" answer, the Universe can often give you the sign you need. You can ask for help with anything you're struggling with—relationships, finances, health, sadness—and you can always ask for encouragement that you're heading in the right direction.

COMMON SIGNS FROM THE UNIVERSE

- Finding coins
- Hearing meaningful music
- Seeing animals and birds
- Repeating numbers
- Finding feathers

Even when you receive your sign, however, you may still doubt that it's a sign just for you. When I was trying to decide if I should leave my safe, happy teaching job, I asked the Universe for a sign to let me know if I was really meant to leave my secure career to focus on readings and metaphysical instruction. I was walking home from my neighborhood book club one evening, thinking about how huge and scary this decision felt. What would people say? How could I walk away from a retirement plan and benefits? What was I thinking? Standing in the middle of my street facing my home, I said aloud to the night sky: "Please show me a clear sign if I should take this leap of faith." Suddenly, a shooting star passed over my house. I gasped. A sign! A clear sign just for me!

But as I walked into my house, I was already doubting it. How many millions of people all over the world just saw that very same shooting star? I told myself that I was grasping for anything to make me feel better about this big decision. The next morning, I prayed for a more specific sign that was just for me to let me know if I should do this. I added: "If I don't receive a sign today, I will know that I'm supposed to stay at the college teaching."

After a long day of teaching, I met my friend for our daily late-afternoon walk. She was chatting about her day when something nudged me to look up. I stopped in awe and wonder as a small white feather wafted back and forth as it fell from the sky. I held out my hand and waited as the feather fell gently into my palm. I still have that white feather sitting atop a bowl of crystals on my bedside table to serve as a reminder that I'm right where I'm supposed to be.

It's okay to doubt and test the signs you receive from the Universe because you must be sure that you're receiving the guidance you requested. One listener recently shared a beautiful sign she received twice after testing the response to a request she had made.

I've been asking for signs from the Universe to help me know if my family and I are ready for twins. As I will need fertility treatments, twins are a real possibility. I asked to see a double rainbow to let me know. The next day, my family and I were returning from a beautiful day in the countryside, with not a drop of rain in sight. But suddenly my husband said: "Look! A double rainbow!" I wondered whether this could really be a sign for me. We were all seeing this double rainbow.

So that night, I asked for a more personal sign that was just for me. The next day, I went to buy a book for my niece. As I went to the check-out, the cashier took out a little key chain from behind the desk and said: "I don't know why, but I feel you need this." When I read it, I almost cried with joy. The key chain said: "Double-rainbow power." I couldn't doubt the sign any longer.

Synchronicities and Symbols

The Universe loves to communicate with us through synchronicities and symbols. Anytime you receive a repeated message in unusual ways that make you take notice, you are receiving a message from the Universe. A friend of mine recently sold her business and is trying to determine what the next chapter of her life will look like. After my mom died, my friend came over to help us pack up her things. She held up a small crystalline oyster with a pearl inside and said: "That's weird. I keep getting the message 'The world is your oyster.' I'd never heard that expression before. But it was written on a card someone sent me. Then a friend said it me, and now I find this." I told her to keep it as a reminder that the Universe was nudging her to embrace this happy new chapter of her life.

I often receive books as a message from the Universe. When I was trying to connect more with angels, I found a book at my local metaphysical store that focused on meeting your guardian angel. I brought it up to the register and was surprised when the owner said: "This isn't one of my books. I buy every item in this store, and I've never seen this book. Look—it doesn't even have my price sticker on it." I didn't know what to say, so I offered her twenty dollars for the book. She smiled and answered: "No way. Clearly this book is meant for you, so just take it."

When I was writing my last book and felt stuck at one point in my writing process, I walked away from my laptop and headed to my local bookstore for inspiration. I always think better when I'm surrounded by books. I ordered a cup of tea and was sitting down on a little bench with my notebook when I heard a thud. A book had fallen off the shelf all by itself. It was a book on dreams by Robert Moss and contained all the inspiration I needed to finish my chapter.

Often the Universe will speak to us through symbols like animals or numbers. When my friend was struggling with trying to get pregnant, a rabbit began appearing every morning in her backyard. I told her that rabbits are a sign of fertility and that this was the Universe's way of telling her to relax, because she'd be pregnant in no time. She received a positive pregnancy test three weeks later and never saw that rabbit in her yard again.

Repeating numbers are also a common way the Universe talks to us. A listener shared this message she received about numbers.

As I have recently started my consciousness journey, I wanted to have a sign that I am on the right path. Shortly after, I began seeing the numbers 11:11 and 1:11 or receiving $11.11 in change. I continued to ask for a sign, until one night, someone came to me in my dream and said: "We are showing you numbers!"

I instantly woke up and looked at the clock. It was
11:11.

She finally realized how silly it was not to have noticed
the signs before.

One student emailed wondering why the Universe
was showing her 777 over and over. Twice in one week
she'd received $7.77 in change. The next week when she
traveled for work, her flight was number 777. When she
ordered Chinese food and opened her fortune cookie, it
said her lucky number was 777. I told her that 7 is a number that has long been revered as mystical; it asks us to
meditate and seek answers within. There are seven notes
on a musical scale, seven days in a week, seven colors in
the rainbow, and seven chakras. Each phase of the moon
lasts seven days. The ancient Egyptians taught that there
were seven paths to heaven, while Christians believe God
rested on the seventh day after creating the world.

But as I typed my response to her, I kept seeing three
sevens with cherries popping up in alignment on a slot
machine. So I added: "Triple seven can also be a lucky
number. Maybe the Universe is trying to tell you you're
coming into some good luck." She took that message to
heart and bought a lottery ticket called Lucky 7s at her
local convenience store—and won $5,000.

The Universe also speaks to us through repeating messages that we often write off as coincidences. When I was
thinking of starting a podcast, I was afraid to put myself

out there. It was one thing to teach metaphysical classes in my hometown, but it felt much scarier to broadcast my ideas to a wider audience. Each time I meditated on this decision, I saw the familiar commercial tagline "Just Do It." Soon I started seeing this message everywhere—on bumper stickers, on posters at my gym, and in ads in magazines. When I was waiting in line at a store, I overheard two women talking behind me. One was telling her friend: "Oh Haley, just do it. You know you're ready." This is a common way the Universe tries to talk to us. If you overhear a conversation that seems to match exactly what you need to hear, or if a friend feels compelled out of the blue to repeat a message you've been receiving through your prayers and meditations, take this as a sign from the Universe.

You have many tools at your disposal to help you recognize and read the messages the Universe is sending you—among them meditation, crystals, oracle cards, journaling, pendulums, and prayer. These tools all center on learning how to still the noise of living in your busy world so you can tune in to your own heart and listen to the guidance waiting to be heard. Let's take a brief look at each one.

Meditation

Perhaps the best tool you have for communicating with the Universe is meditation. Any time you spend in quiet interior reflection and silence—whether it's five minutes in the morning, twenty minutes on your lunch break, or an hour before bedtime—will help you feel at one with your soul, with the Universe, with the collective unconscious, and with your team of allies.

Meditation has been proven to have beneficial effects on physical, emotional, and spiritual health. It helps reduce stress, improves sleep, and focuses attention. It's also been shown to help reduce anxiety, increase dream recall, and even lower blood pressure. When you take time to meditate, you cultivate an energy of receptivity that allows you to become a vessel for insight, answers, and guidance. In that sense, meditating is like the needle on a compass that points you in the right direction.

There are several ways to meditate, and no one way is better than another. In active meditation, you walk alone listening to the sounds around you and allow your inner voice to be silent and still. You can actively meditate while doing anything repetitive, like knitting, washing dishes, or running. The practice of focusing your physical self on a repetitive task stills the chaos that so often reigns in your egoic mind and allows your soul to break through and connect with your consciousness. In guided meditation, you listen to someone leading you through a series of visualizations with the aim of relaxing your body and helping your soul seek answers to a concern or question you pose prior to the meditation.

A simple way to meditate is to sit in silence and find a point of focus, like counting your breaths, or gazing at a candle flame, or repeating a mantra. Your goal is to concentrate on this focal point until you're no longer aware of it, ultimately reaching a state where you're not focusing on anything at all. Don't resist thoughts that pop into your head. Allow them to enter and gently leave your mind, Then return to your focal point. Repeat this process for five minutes each day, gradually working your way up to ten minutes and then fifteen.

Ideally, you should meditate for about thirty minutes a day. But any time you can find to slow down, sit in silence, and focus your mind on going within will reap huge rewards for you.

Crystals

Crystals are a fantastic way to slow down an overthinking mind and learn to master the beauty of silence and meditation. These gifts from the Earth can help increase your vibrations, open your Third Eye, protect your spiritual energy, and charge up a room with positive vibes.

Crystals have been used throughout the ages as talismans for protection, adornments in temples, and symbols of loyalty in love. They are used today to power watches and computers, but they can also be used to jump-start your intuition. Crystals work within your auric field and serve as conduits for energy flow. Lapis lazuli, labradorite, amethyst, or clear quartz are wonderful stones to use in meditation. When you wear or carry crystals with you, they sync with your energetic field and help you awaken to your intuition.

Crystals are also a great tool for balancing energy. Each crystal vibrates at its own frequency. When you bring a crystal into your unique energy field, it helps synchronize your vibration with its own. The vibration of a stone is constant, whereas your vibratory frequency is constantly fluctuating. Sometimes you feel happy and energized; sometimes you feel low and run-down. When you bring a high-vibrating crystal into your energy field, it works to match your energy with its own high vibration, helping you to feel more focused and energized. If you're feeling anxious, you can work with a lower-vibrating crystal to help calm your overactive mind.

Crystals help you adapt your electromagnetic field to their vibration. When you work with a high-vibration stone like clear quartz, your electromagnetic field increases. When you work with a lower-vibrating stone like hematite, your electromagnetic field slows and calms down. The structure of a crystal grows in perfect harmony, whereas you tend to bend and sway with the energies of those around you. But crystals help to bring your energy into alignment. If crystals can help a watch keep time or a computer store energy, then possibly they can help you on your road to healing. Some research has even shown that crystal patterns actually take on the shape of what you are thinking about. Scientists suggest that this may be the result of vibrations that connect your molecules with those of a crystal.

Crystals can receive, hold, direct, project, and reflect light. If you hold or carry a crystal with you for a few weeks, it brings you into alignment with its vibration and helps you to center and balance your own energy. Crystals hold and emanate light and have been witnessed to help align energy, so it's reasonable to assume that they can also help you to take in more light and focus on hearing the still, small voice within you.

Different crystals have different properties and vibrations. Clear quartz helps expand and increase your energy. Rose quartz helps you receive more love. Jasper is great for grounding and protection. In general, the color of the stone tells you a lot about its main purpose. Pink stones help with love. Green stones facilitate growth, healing, and abundance. Orange crystals are wonderful for fertility and creativity. Yellow stones increase joyfulness and confidence. Black stones provide protection. Purple stones connect you with the divine.

Once you've chosen a crystal to help with your specific need, hold it in your hand and visualize white light flowing into your crown chakra and down through your head, neck, chest, and arms, and out into your hands, filling your crystal with light. Then state your intention for your crystal.

For example, if you're using black tourmaline to protect your energy, say: "I ask that you be a protective crystal for me, always working to shield me from taking on the negativity of others. Thank you." If you're working with a green prehnite crystal to enhance your healing, say: "It is my intent that you be my healing crystal. Whenever I wear you, please work to heal, balance, and cleanse my energy. Thank you." If you're using rose quartz to attract love, say: "I ask that you heal my heart and open my soul to receive true love. Thank you." Say what comes naturally to you. Then continue to hold your crystal while beaming white light into it for several more minutes.

Hold the crystal in your palms when you meditate. Carry it with you or sleep with it under your pillow to aid in dream recall and to make you more receptive to messages from the Universe.

Oracle Cards

People have looked for answers in the cards throughout history. The Tarot dates back to the 15th century, and has been used across many cultures to help people predict and interpret events. Today, there are oracle decks based on everything from angels to animals, and from Rumi to Jane Austin. Even our normal deck of playing cards has its origins in the Tarot, with the suits deriving from the Minor Arcana—pentacles becoming diamonds, swords becoming spades, cups becoming hearts, and wands becoming clubs.

There are several traditional spreads to choose from when using oracle cards, like the Tree of Life spread or the Celtic Cross spread. One of the simpler spreads that is good for beginners is a Past, Present, Future reading in which you simply shuffle the deck while thinking of your question and then pull three cards. The first represents the past; the second signifies the present; the third points to future outcomes. This spread can help you get out of your own way and put you in touch with your higher self and inner guidance. A great way to learn how to use an oracle deck is simply to ask each morning: "What do I need to know today?" Then pick a card to symbolize your day.

Journaling

Journaling helps you acknowedge your innermost thoughts, and gives them the chance to be seen, heard, expressed, and released. When you journal, you give yourself permission to communicate your worries, anxieties, fears, hopes, and dreams. Journaling has been proven to help inspire more creativity and critical thinking. It enables you to process your emotions in a safe, nonjudgmental environment. Exploring your interior world in this way helps you get in touch with your true desires, needs, and wants.

Often just the act of writing down a fear or worry is enough to release it. Use your journal as a way of communicating with the Universe. Write: "Dear Universe, what do I need to know today?" Then place the pen in your non-dominant hand and allow the answers to flow across your page.

Pendulums

A pendulum is a small weight suspended on chain that allows you to connect directly to your subconscious. They have been used throughout history to find water, locate gold, and unearth treasures. During World War II, pendulums were used to locate hidden bombs. Miners in South Africa use them to find precious minerals. How do they work? When you pose a question, your subconscious responds through your nervous system. These reactions are communicated, through the nerve endings in your fingers, to the chain holding the pendulum.

Most pendulums found in metaphysical stores today are made from some kind of crystal hanging on a chain. But you can make your own pendulum by simply knotting a string through a button. If you find a stone or shell with a hole in it, you can use this to make your own unique pendulum.

Pendulums give "yes," "no," and "maybe/don't know" answers. Once you get your pendulum, hold it in your hand. Allow the top three inches of the chain to drape over your fingers as you hold it dangling between your thumb and forefinger. Ask the pendulum to show you a "yes" answer, then wait patiently for it to move. It should start to swing gently back and forth. Note the direction in which it moves to signify "yes." Then ask it to show you a "no" answer and note the direction it moves. Finally, ask it to show you a "maybe" or "don't know" answer. Usually for this one, it will simply stop swinging or it will move in a circle.

Once your pendulum has shown you how it will move for specific answers, test it to make sure you're engaging it properly. Ask it questions to which you know the answer is "yes," like: "Am I holding this pendulum?" Then ask questions the answers to which you know are false, like: "Is the sky yellow?" Keep practicing with your pendulum until you have calibrated its movements.

Most crystals move in one of four ways: up and down, left and right, in a circle, or dancing at the end of the chain—often called "bobbing." Sometimes when a pendulum bobs it means that the answer is still unknown. If the pendulum swings quickly, it indicates a strong energy surrounding the question. If it moves only a little, it usually represents waning energy or that the answer could change. If the pendulum's swing increases—for example, if it's moving in a circle and the arc gets bigger and bigger—it means the energy around the question is developing.

Working with pendulums can be a great way to get guidance for yourself when your ego is getting in the way of your intuition.

Prayer

The word "prayer" comes from the Latin word *precari*, which means "to ask." But as I often remind my children, God/Goddess/Source is not a wishing well. Prayer is about taking time out of your day to tune in and check in with yourself and your higher power. It establishes an intimate relationship with God. Imagine being married to someone and never once speaking to that person. It wouldn't be much of a marriage, would it? Yet that's how many of us go through life—wanting a deeper connection with our higher power, but never taking the time to communicate with it. But when you make prayer a part of your daily life—like brushing your teeth and checking your email—you find yourself feeling calmer, less stressed, more guided and connected. And miracles start to occur in your life.

There are four steps to keep in mind when practicing daily prayer—prepare, request, affirm, and yield. They are easy to remember with the acronym PRAY.

- **Prepare:** Preparing for prayer means taking time out to check within. How are you feeling about the different situations in your life? Is something nagging at you? Are you feeling guilty? Has someone hurt your feelings? Take an inventory of your emotions and share these with your higher power. Center yourself by taking deep, calming breaths. Fill your body with the light of God's love while reflecting on the divine energy that is a part of you. When you pray, you enter sacred space. Prepare your heart and soul for this.

- **Request:** Tell your higher power what you would like to occur in your life this day. Include friends, family members, and co-workers for whom you'd like to pray as well. Prayer is simply thought-directed energy. So when you pray for someone else, you send them good energy. Try to make your prayer request as specific as possible. Don't make the change you're asking for be the responsibility of others; make it your own. If, for example, you're dealing with a difficult boss, instead of praying for your boss to change, pray that God works through your heart so that you're able to understand and work well with this person.

- **Affirm:** Since prayer is energy, when you repeat a prayer or affirmation over and over, it reinforces a chemical pathway in the brain. Pagans knot a string nine times to lock in the energy of a prayer request, while Catholics say Novenas for nine days—a tradition that began before Christ ascended and asked his apostles to pray for nine days until Pentecost when the Holy Spirit descended. Throughout many religious traditions, repeating and affirming prayers has been shown to help significantly. Affirming your prayer repeatedly also helps you to focus energy and attract what you are seeking.

- **Yield:** This is probably the most important and hardest part of the praying process. You must yield to your higher power's answer and be ready to receive a "no." The Universe always answers your prayers. Always. It's just that sometimes the answer is "yes," and sometimes it's "no" or "not now." Being ready to yield to the answer you receive takes an attitude of trust and surrender, and a deep belief in the infinite wisdom of the Universe.

Living from the Heart

In order to be a co-designer and co-creator of the Universe, you need to ask for specific signs in a timely manner, be open to seeing them in unusual ways, and maintain an observant awareness of them as they occur around you. The best tool you have at your disposal for this is your own beautiful heart. This is where your soul resides.

When you point at yourself or someone motions to you, think about where that finger points—right at the heart. When you identify yourself to others, you never point to your head. You always point to your heart. This is because you know intuitively that your soul lives in your heart center. This is where all the magic of being a successful co-creator and spiritually attuned person happens. Your heart knows the way.

It's been said that the greatest distance we ever travel is from our heads to our hearts. Too often, we oblige the anxious ramblings of our minds, when truly all we need to know is waiting to be discovered within our hearts.

One of the best ways to listen to the whispers of your heart is to sit quietly and write down everything that's on your mind. Get it all down on paper—all your worries, anxieties, and upcoming tasks. When you've finished, rip this paper up and throw it away. Then sit in a comfortable position and place both hands over your heart and take several deep, centering breaths. Feel your chest expand and your heart awaken with each inhale. Visualize yourself sitting in the center of your heart. Sit in the silence and peace of this moment and allow your heart to speak to you.

While crystals, meditation, and other metaphysical tools can help you connect within to expand your wisdom and realize your fullest potential, the best way to tune into your soul plan is by living from the heart. You have this one beautiful life in this one particular moment and place on Earth to experience, cultivate, and share the wondrous essence that is you. Don't waste this gift of life by living in fear or following someone else's dream or fulfilling a family member's expectation of who you should be. You are a divine being, created in love, who's been given this time on Earth to light it up in a glorious way that's unique to you and your talents, your gifts, and your perfect expression.

But the only way to share your light is to live from a place of truth. Who are you right now? In this moment? What do you want most in the world? How do you want to share your light with others? What wisdom will you leave behind when it's your time to return home?

When you are able to chip away at the layers of society's projections, generational karma, family labels, and your own misconceived notions regarding your true gifts, you reveal your authentic self. And this is when the magic really happens. This is when you are able to take up the reins of your life and navigate the course of your journey away from the rat race of competition and material success toward one that is imbued with peace, compassion, gratitude, and truth.

There are many ways you can connect with the divine to obtain the wisdom, guidance, and insight you need to help you remember who you are and why you're here. You can meet the divine on your knees in surrender, on the cross of suffering, or standing on your own two feet staring into the mirror. When you learn the secret language of the Universe, you learn to embrace your authentic self and live from the heart. You cultivate the courage you need to stand in your truth and claim your divine right to happiness, abundance, and love in all its beautiful expressions.

Light Lessons: Your Mission Statement

This exercise is designed to help you connect to your authentic self by writing your own personal mission statement. In the world of business, mission statements usually consist of one concise sentence that reflects the aims, goal, and values of a company. This exercise requires that you think about your life, your goals, and your values, and then put them into one sentence that states what you see as your soul's mission in life.

When writing this statement, consider these points:

- It should reflect every aspect of the life goals you wish to accomplish.
- It should be written in the present tense.
- It should be no longer than one sentence.
- It should reflect your special talents and any attributes that you have or wish to have.

Consider these questions as you write your mission statement:

- What do you want your life to look like in one year?
- What gifts and talents do you have to offer the world?
- What role will family and friends play in your mission?
- What kind of relationships do you need to foster to see your goals become reality?
- What underlying philosophies about life will guide your success?
- How will others benefit from your mission?

Once you've completed your mission statement, walk away from it for a day or two, then come back to it and see if it needs to be tweaked. When your mission statement is completed, paste it somewhere where you will see it every day—on your laptop, in your office, on the refrigerator. Look at it often and affirm that you are living your soul purpose.

CONCLUSION: GRADUATION DAY

Dear Soul,

Congratulations on completing your course of study at the University of Life. You have been divinely guided to sit in this moment of awareness right now, looking within and contemplating where you want your seeker's heart to guide you next. Now it's time to answer the call of your soul, to live from your heart and share your light in the unique, beautiful way only you can. Remember to seek worth not wealth, love not lust, patience not perfection, compassion not competition, respect not recognition, serenity not success, courage not comfort. For when you own your authentic self, all the lure of winning at life loosens its grip on you and you find that what remains is joy, freedom, and peace.

Everything in this school of Earth is temporary. Joy. Pain. Success. Losing. Winning. It's all fleeting. And through it all, only two things remain constant—love and fear. Choose love in all your fleeting moments and allow your soul to soar to new heights. What will your life look like when you allow love, not fear, to be in charge? Fear reacts. Courage acts.

Now is the time to act on your dreams and invest in self-love, so you can unleash the divine co-creator within you. Shine your light so brightly that it illuminates the world around you and within you. You are meant to create and inspire love. Magic and miracles occur when you remember to be the light—both for yourself and others.

You are the answer. You are the writer of your soul plan. You are the light.

APPENDIX A: INDEX OF EXERCISES

BIBLIOGRAPHY

Andrews, Ted. *How to Meet and Work With Your Spirit Guides*. MN: Llewellyn Publications, 2006.

Aristotle. *Aristotle's Nicomachean Ethics*. IL: University of Chicago Press, 2012.

Campbell, Joseph. *The Hero With a Thousand Faces: The Collected Works of Joseph Campbell*. CA: New World Library, 2008.

Crum, Alia J., and Ellen J. Langer. "Mind-Set Matters." *Psychological Science*, vol. 18, no. 2, Feb. 2007, pp. 165–171.

Dante Alighieri. *The Divine Comedy of Dante Alighieri : Inferno, Purgatory, Paradise*. NY: The Union Library Association, 1935.

Hesiod. *Theogony and Works and Days*. UK: Oxford University Press, 2009.

Jarrow, Rick. *Creating the Work You Love: Courage, Commitment and Career*. NY: Destiny Books, 1995.

Jung, Carl. *Memories, Dreams and Reflections*. NY: Vintage Books, 1989.

Newton, Michael. *Journey of Souls*. MN: Llewellyn Publications, 1994.

McTaggart, Lynne. *The Power of Eight: Harnessing the Miraculous Energies of a Small Group to Heal Others, Your Life, and the World*. NY: Atria Books, 2017.

Melody, *Love Is in the Earth: A Kaleidoscope of Crystals: The Reference Book Describing the Metaphysical Properties of the Mineral Kingdom*. CO: Earth, Love Publications, 1995.

Mitchell, Stephen. *The Enlightened Heart: An Anthology of Sacred Poetry*. NY: Harper Perennial, 1993.

Pagels, Elaine. *Beyond Belief: The Secret Gospel of Thomas*. NY: Vintage Books, 2004.

Plato, Aristophanes, Thomas West. *Four Texts on Socrates*. NY: Cornell University Press, 1998.

Radin, Dean. *Real Magic: Ancient Wisdom, Modern Science, and a Guide to the Secret Power of the Universe*. NY: Harmony Books. 2018.

Tales of Everyday Magic: My Greatest Teacher. Directed by Michael
    Goorjian. Performances by Patrick Fabian and Wayne Dyer. Hay
    House, 2012.

Shinn, Florence Scovil. *The Complete Works of Florence Scovil Shinn.* FL:
    Mockingbird Press, 2021.

Webster, Richard. *Guardian Angels: How to Contact and Work with
    Angelic Protectors.* MN: Llewellyn Publications, 2022.

_____. *Spirit Guides and Angel Guardians: Contact Your Invisible
    Helpers.* MN: Llewellyn Publications, 2002.

ABOUT THE AUTHOR

Samantha Fey is the cohost of two popular podcasts, *Psychic Teachers* and *Enlightened Empaths*, that teach listeners how to embrace and celebrate their innate sensitivity and gifts. Her work has been featured on *Beyond Belief* with George Noory, *Coast to Coast AM*, and *Woman's World*, and she's a frequent presenter at Edgar Cayce's A.R.E. After earning her master's degree in education, she taught English for many years and now writes and teaches about crystals, Reiki, healing, and intuition. She's the author of *The Awake Dreamer: A Guide to Lucid Dreaming, Astral Travel, and Mastering the Dreamscape*. For more information, go to her web site at *samanthafey.com*.